THE ELEMENTS OF THE ARTHURIAN TRADITION

John Matthews has spent more than twenty years studying and writing about King Arthur and his Knights, their families, friends and enemies. An important aspect of his approach is the value of personal involvement on the part of those who read or study the tradition. He is the author of many books on the Arthurian Legends, and whilst continuing to explore the work himself, he gives lectures and runs workshops both in Europe and America.

The *Elements Of* is a series designed to present high quality introductions to a broad range of essential subjects.

The books are commissioned specifically from experts in their fields. They provide readable and often unique views of the various topics covered, and are therefore of interest both to those who have some knowledge of the subject, as well as those who are approaching it for the first time.

Many of these concise yet comprehensive books have practical suggestions and exercises which allow personal experience as well as theoretical understanding, and offer a valuable source of information on many important themes.

In the same series

The Aborigine Tradition	The I Ching
Alchemy	Islam
Astrology	Judaism
The Bahá'í Faith	Meditation
Buddhism	Mysticism
Celtic Christianity	Native American Traditions
The Celtic Tradition	Natural Magic
The Chakras	Numerology
Christian Symbolism	Pendulum Dowsing
Creation Myth	Prophecy
Dreamwork	Psychosynthesis
The Druid Tradition	The Qabalah
Earth Mysteries	Reincarnation
The Egyptian Wisdom	The Runes
Feng Shui	Shamanism
Gnosticism	Sufism
The Goddess	Tai Chi
The Grail Tradition	Taoism
Graphology	The Tarot
Handreading	Visualisation
Herbalism	Yoga
Hinduism	Zen
Human Potential	

> the elements of

the arthurian tradition

john matthews

ELEMENT

Shaftesbury, Dorset · Rockport, Massachusetts · Brisbane, Queensland

© John Matthews 1989

First published in Great Britain in 1989 by
Element Books Limited
Shaftesbury, Dorset SP7 8BP

Published in the USA in 1991 by
Element Books, Inc.
PO Box 830, Rockport, MA 01966

Published in Australia in 1991 by
Element Books Limited for
Jacaranda Wiley Limited
33 Park Road, Milton, Brisbane 4064

Reprinted September 1989
Reprinted 1991
Reprinted 1992
Reprinted February and June 1993
Reprinted 1995
Reprinted 1996

Designed by Jenny Liddle
Cover design by Max Fairbrother
Typeset by Selectmove Limited, London
Printed and bound in Great Britain by
Biddles Limited, Guildford & King's Lynn

British Library Cataloguing in Publication Data
Matthews, John *1948–*
The elements of the arthurian tradition.
1. Legends, Characters, Arthur, King
I. Title
398′.352

Library of Congress Cataloging in Publication
data available

ISBN 1–85230–074–4

To
John Boorman
for keeping the tradition alive

THE ARTHURIAN EPIC CYCLUS
According to the narrative of
The Anglo-Norman Trouvères

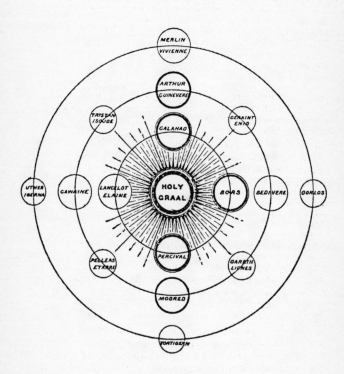

THE KING'S MOON-RITE

(For David Jones)

From the mounds of Crooked Back there came
but three common men: Morvran mab Tegid
who for his ugliness no man would strike;
Sendaf Bright-Angel, who for his beauty
death forfend; and Glewlwyd Mighty-Grasp
whose strength none might withstand . . .

And these three through the field walked arm in arm
as Logres-In-Britain crumbled into darkness again,
and once again dreams rode in the land –
of the one who struck the Grievous Blow
(the Red man from the Lake);
of he who forbore to ask the question;
and, of the Ship of Glass that never sailed
but rode the shape of Bardsey –
while the Bear went out in Prydwen
to rifle Hell and come again
with gifts for all who still held true . . .

He is remembered in the stars – Arcturus and Telyn Idris –
and the mountains do not forget
the debt of Crooked Bank.
But the Head of Bran no longer stares above Lud's Town,
Nor is it known who lay in need: King Pellam
Lord of Lystenesse, or the Crow with Singing Head.

But she who waits beyond the water, watches all,
crooning to her Poet-Lover, caught within the bush;
and who has seen her floating on the water's moonlit silver,
that has not also heard her siren song;
and who has seen the Cup flame in the West
that has not also seen the breath of Nine
smoke on the air to warm the Cauldron's rim;
and who has seen the Table that has not also seen it
crack as men rode over it with plunging hooves of steel –
to scatter the titled chairs in which the Hosts had sat . . .

The Sword went down in water, shaken and drowned.
The Sword was named Escalibor, the Spear Rhongomyniad,
The Mantle of Brightness Gwern.
But he who was both King and Dux, Director of Toil, Amherawdr,
Lord of the Wave in ancestral purple,
walking in the Waste,
sits yet upon his golden chair, his hair and beard grown long.
And leads the Hounds of Annwn over the height of moor and peak.
And in the caves he sleeps, the Bear, the Crow, the Saturnine Lord,
and casts a silver horseshoe on Saint John's Eve,
and guards the Burning Tree for better days.

John Matthews

CONTENTS

Acknowledgements   xi

Introduction: What is the Arthurian Tradition?   xii

1. The High King: Arthur in History and Myth   1

2. Merlin and the Prophecies of the Land:

   Vision and Enchantment at Camelot   13

3. The Round Table: Adventure in the Forest of the Mind   27

4. Goddesses and Guides:

   Morgan le Fay and the Otherworldly Women   38

5. Lancelot and Tristan: True Love and Perfect Chivalry   48

6. The Grail Quest: Spirituality and the Search for Absolutes   62

7. Avalon and the Faery Realms: Paths to the Land Beyond   74

8. The Unending Song: Arthur in the Modern World   84

Exercises:

1. The Starry King   11

2. Merlin's Tower   24

3. The Table Round   35

4. Finding a Guide   46
5. The Cave of the Heart   60
6. The Chapel of the Grail   72
7. The Isle of Dreams   81
8. The Future King   92

Glossary of Arthurian Characters   94
Bibliography   105
Index   110

ACKNOWLEDGEMENTS

To Gareth Knight, with whom I first learned how the Arthurian tradition could be applied to daily living.

To Bob Stewart for the many rewarding hours of conversation which helped clarify much that was mysterious.

To my wife, Caitlín Matthews, for her continuing support, and for helping me to explore new dimensions.

To my son, Emrys, for patiently waiting until I had finished my work before I could come and play.

To Chesca Potter for supplying a missing piece in the puzzle.

To the Colleagues of my 'other' life, who put up with my moods when things went wrong.

To the legion of writers who paved the way, and to whom I wish I could offer acknowledgement individually.

INTRODUCTION

WHAT IS THE ARTHURIAN TRADITION?

Stories of adventure, of magic and romance are the stuff of the Arthurian tradition, which draws its energy from many sources. From the intricately woven fabric of Celtic myth and legend came the tales of Arthur and Avalon, of Merlin and the Grail, of the Otherworldly women who were its guardians. From the great chivalric epics of the Middle Ages came the stories of the Round Table knights: Lancelot and Galahad, Perceval and Gareth, Gawain and Lamorack, whose adventures filled literally thousands of manuscript pages relating their journeys through the dark, impenetrable forests of the Arthurian world. From the complex ethic of Courtly Love, defined like a religious code, came a new attitude to women, who were no longer seen as chattels to be bought and sold in the matrimonial market-place of feudal Europe, but as potential goddesses all. This gave rise to unforgettable women such as Guinevere, Isolde, Elaine of Astolat and Dindraine, and to the legion of ladies wooed and won, rescued and championed, by the knights who loved them.

And behind all this, underpinning the whole mighty structure, lay a deeper dimension, drawn from a heritage of magical tradition, seeded by countless generations until it burst forth in the flowering of literature throughout the Middle Ages. Here the themes which had dominated the inner lives of mankind from the Dreamtime before history found a place. The eternal interaction of the Otherworld with our own dimension forms a constant backdrop to the tales of Arthur and his heroes, their loves and their adventures. The secrets of immortality, of harmony with the earth, of true love and spiritual fulfilment, were only some of the rich gifts offered to these wandering men and women, who appear and disappear in an ever more bewildering fashion in the thronging scenes of countless texts.

Strange and terrible were the adventures they undertook with a merry heart; strange and terrible also were their adversaries: shape shifting magicians and enchantresses, wild beasts possessed of intelligence greater than that of their kind, serpents that turned into beautiful women if anyone dared to kiss them, invisible foes who struck from nowhere, demons and ghosts and knights whose armour changed colour in the blink of an eye. Even the landscape itself seemed unearthly, with its underwater bridges, fountains which boiled or ran with blood, trees one half in flame and the other in green leaf, wasted lands which grew green again at a single word.

Magical weapons, magic rings, horses and bridles, swords pulled from stones that floated on water, ships that sailed by themselves and chess pieces moved by unseen hands – these are but a few of the elements which go to make up the world of the Arthurian tradition. Some we will meet in these pages, others we may seek out for ourselves among the countless tales which make up the 'Matter of Britain'.

Above all it should be recognised that these are not simply stories. Within them lies a depth and variety of human experience which derives from a timeless dimension. Taken as part of the continuing Western mystery tradition, they form a background to daily living in a unique and extraordinary way. All myths are timeless and cannot be defined or pigeon-holed to suit individual inclination. Yet they are for all, as that wise mythographer Pamela Travers noted:

> The myths never have a single meaning, once and for all and finished. They have something greater; they have meaning itself. If you hang a crystal sphere in the window it will give off light from all parts of itself. That is how the myths are; they have a meaning for me, for you, and for everyone else.[84]

Thus the Arthurian tradition too is for everyone who cares to explore it. Nor should their involvement stop short with a mere reading of the texts – rewarding though that can be. Deeper, more experiential levels can be reached by working with the Arthurian archetypes in an imaginative way. Some suggestions as to the ways in which this can be achieved will be found throughout this book. Those who attempt these exercises are assured of a wholly new and developing dimension in their lives, for within these stories lies a heritage for the future of all who seek it.

Finally, while I have ranged widely among the multitude of Arthurian texts, one in particular has been central to the creation of this book. This is Sir Thomas Malory's great work *Le Morte D'Arthur*,[47] which as a late work, written in 1485, not only sums up much of what had gone before, but also makes it accessible. Malory's uniqueness lies in his individuality and independence, which gave him the freedom to shape and adapt the stories which went into the making of his book according to a personal vision of the 'high order of Chivalry'. He is also a great stylist, whose words are often unforgettably poignant and charged.

Throughout this book therefore I have taken Malory as a primary source and have not hesitated to paraphrase his words as though they were my own. However, since this is not a study of Malory, I have endeavoured to make what follows in the nature of a meditation on, rather than a history of, the subject. Those wishing to go more deeply into the question of the Arthurian tradition can still do no better than read Malory, supplemented by the romances of Chrétien de Troyes[8] the *Mabinogion*[46] and the English Gawain cycle.[23] Other, less familiar works, are referred to at appropriate points in the text, or in the bibliography at the end of the book. However, the emphasis throughout has been on the imaginal dimension, since this still remains a vital part of what is, to this day, a *living* tradition.

1 · THE HIGH KING:

ARTHUR IN HISTORY AND MYTH

Whither has not flying fame spread and familiarized the name of Arthur the Briton, even as far as the empire of Christendom extends? Who, I say, does not speak of Arthur the Briton, since he is almost better known to the peoples of Asia than to the *Britanni* (Welsh and Cornish), as our palmers returning from the East inform us? The Eastern peoples speak of him, as do the Western, though separated by the width of the whole earth .... Rome, queen of cities, sings his deeds, nor are Arthur's wars unknown to her former rival Carthage. Antioch, Armenia, Palestine celebrate his acts.

Alanus de Insulis

THE CELTIC HERO

Arthur is a Celtic hero and it is as a Celt and thus part of the Celtic world that he should be seen. No matter how far removed in time and culture the stories may take him, we should never allow ourselves to forget that they were a product of that society, and that this point of origin continued to be felt long after Arthur had become recognised as a Christian king in shining armour with a band of heroes who met at a Round Table and spent their times in pursuit of adventure and love.

Arthur's historical origins are, as we would expect, themselves shrouded in myth. The legends tell that he was the son of King

Uther Pendragon and the Lady Igraine of Cornwall, and that his birth was made possible through the magical arts of the magician Merlin, who later became his advisor in all things. History allows him no such romantic heritage; it grants him no known parents, no wizard counsellor, no band of shining knights. What it does suggest is in its own way just as remarkable.

Arthur was born, so far as we can tell, sometime in the fifth or sixth century, either in Wales, the Midlands or Cornwall, and he became, not a great king, but an equally great war-leader, with the title *Dux Brittanorum*, Duke of Britain. As such he commanded the armies of the various petty kings and chieftains who had reasserted their claims to the land after the last vestiges of Roman rule came to an end in the previous century. Endlessly quarrelling, continuously raiding each other's lands for the sheer sport of it, they would have fallen easy victims to incoming invaders from Germany and Freisia, had it not been for Arthur, who persuaded the warring factions to fight against a common foe and to place him at the head of an army drawn from every quarter of the land.

How he did so is not recorded, as indeed are few of his subsequent deeds. He seems to have led a band of mounted cavalry, perhaps the original 'Knights of the Round Table', whose mobility enabled them to strike deep into the territory overrun by their enemies, withdraw as swiftly as they had come, and appear again many miles distant to strike at another foe. Such tactics – learned, perhaps, from Roman military methods in other lands – must have given Arthur and his men almost magical standing among both their own forces and those of their enemy. And it must have been then that the first stirrings of the legendary tales began to be felt.

Later writers recorded the still-potent presence of Arthur, in the places named after him: Arthur's Seat, Arthur's Stone, Arthur's Oven. A gravestone marked the grave of his son, Anir; if it was moved during one day, the next found it back in its original place. A rocky outcrop bore the print of his hound, Cabal.

A series of great battles was recorded, their sites now difficult if not impossible to identify. In these we hear how Arthur, bearing a shield with the image of the Virgin Mary painted upon it, led his warriors against the Saxons to such good effect that what began as an invasion ended as a more or less peaceful settlement, with the invaders penned within certain areas of the country, where they were able to farm the land and, in time, intermarry – thus founding the people known as the English, a mixture of Celt and Saxon which remained unchanged until the coming of the Normans in the eleventh century.

This was all to have a profound effect on the subsequent history of Arthur, as we shall see, for the Britons who fled the incoming Saxon invaders found sanctuary across the sea in Brittany, opening up a channel which enabled the transmission of tales related orally – including, we must believe, tales about Arthur – which when they returned, in the form of stories and songs told by Anglo-Norman *conteurs* some 500 years later, became the foundation of the medieval romances of Arthur on which most of the tradition is based.

THE ROMANTIC KING

The first writer consciously to draw on the still largely oral sources pertaining to Arthur was a twelfth-century 'historian' named Geoffrey of Monmouth. He it was who created a vehicle for the seemingly inexhaustible supply of stories concerning the exploits of Arthur and his heroes by writing a *History of the Kings of Britain*,[20] which though it deals also with such semi-historical figues as King Lear, Cassivellaunus, and Constantine, allocates more than half the total space to the lives of Arthur and Merlin.

Geoffrey's book became a best-seller of its time, with countless manuscript copies being made and distributed throughout England and the rest of Europe. Although his veracity as an historian was attacked, even by his near-contemporaries, who referred to him as a 'fabulator', a 'writer of lies', there is more than a kernel of truth in what Geoffrey wrote. He claimed to have partially 'translated' an ancient book in the British tongue, although no trace of this has ever been discovered.

Whatever the truth of the matter, there can be no doubt that Geoffrey pulled together strands of oral tradition, of historical memory, and of pure invention, and dressed them in the fashions and settings of the time. In doing so he created the first 'Arthurian' novel, and set the seal upon the literary career of his hero for several ages to follow. Here is part of his description of Arthur's court – from which it will be seen how far we have come from the setting of 'Dark Age' Britain:

> When the feast of Whitsuntide began to draw near, Arthur . . . made up his mind to hold a plenary court at that season and place the crown of the kingdom on his head. He decided, too, to summon to this feast the leaders who owed him homage, so that he could celebrate Whitsun with greater reverence and renew the closest possible pacts of peace with his chieftains . . .

> (trans. L. Thorpe.)

King Arthur and his Knights at the Round Table, from Walter Map, Le Livre des vertueux faix de plusieurs nobles chevaliers, Rouen 1488.

The feast is held at the City of Legions, Caerleon on Usk, and kings and chieftains come from all over Britain, from much of Europe, and from Scandinavia, which Arthur has recently conquered. All attend Mass in two great cathedral churches and afterwards there is a splendid feast, at which Kay the Seneschal, attended by a thousand noblemen dressed in ermine, bore in the food. Geoffrey goes on:

> If I were to describe everything, I should make this story far too long. Indeed, by this time, Britain had reached such a standard of sophistication that it excelled all other kingdoms in its general affluence, the richness of its decorations, and the courteous behaviour of its inhabitants. Every knight in the country who was in any way famed for his bravery wore livery and arms showing his own distinctive colour; and women of fashion often displayed the same colours. They scorned to give their love to any man who had not proved himself three times in battle. In this way the womenfolk became chaste and more virtuous and for their love the knights were ever more daring.
>
> (ibid.)

Already we have here the medieval, Christian court with its knights and ladies, the former seeking to impress the latter with their prowess in battle, its splendid banquets and its great churches. This is no far cry from the romances which were to follow, and which established Arthur as the most important, most widely celebrated king in the Western world.

Geoffrey's work was taken up and translated from the original Latin into both Norman French and Anglo-Saxon. One of these translators, an Anglo-Norman named Wace, added the idea of the Round Table, at which all men sat in equality. A veritable avalanche of Arthurian romances followed, the most famous of which were written, somewhere towards the end of the twelfth century, by a poet from Troyes in France named Chrétien. It is to him that we must look for the boldest conception of the stories which coloured most of the retellings that followed.

From his prolific pen flowed a series of five verse tales: *Erec and Enid*, *Cliges*, *Lancelot*, *Yvain* and *The Story of the Grail*.[8] Within these, much of what we now recognise as the essential core of the Arthurian legends came into being – Chrétien gave us the stories of Arthur's greatest knights, the love affair of Lancelot and Arthur's queen, and the quest for the Grail. Though these must have existed earlier in the form of oral tales, it is to Chrétien that we owe the first written versions.

His work are thronged with Otherwordly or primitive Celtic characters: Edern, son of Nut (Yder), Gilvaethwy, son of Don (Griflet)

5

Gwalchmai (Gawain), who was the Knight of the Goddess, Maelwas (Maheloas) and Guigomar. In *Erec and Enid* it is notable that Arthur is seen as maintaining or reviving the ancient magical custom of the hunt for the White Stag, in which the hero who succeeded in killing the wondrous beast awarded its head to his lady and thus proclaimed her the fairest among all the women of the court. This theme, with its attendant episode of the kiss bestowed upon the winner, harks back to more primitive origins, where the hero married an ancient hag who afterwards transformed herself into a doe, and the hero into a buck.

Even the *Lancelot*, which on one level tells an elaborate and decorous tale of courtly love, in which the hero rescues his mistress from the hands of a desperate man, is based on an earlier Celtic story contained in a sixth-century life of St Gildas, where the protagonist is a lord of the Otherworld who carries off Guinevere, not simply out of desire for her, but because she stands for the Sovereignty of the Land – an ancient notion which saw Arthur as inheriting his kingdom through marriage to an earthly representative of the Goddess.

Three of the stories retold by Chrétien appear in the *Mabinogion*, a collection of ancient Welsh tales collected and written down during the Middle Ages.[46] Debate has raged for a number of years as to which versions are the oldest. It now seems certain that Chrétien wrote his down first, but that whoever the anonymous author of the three tales in the Welsh manuscripts may have been, he almost certainly drew on the same original source as the French Poet, although unlike Chrétien he retained many features of a more primitive nature. These versions of *Erec*, *Yvain*, and *The Story of the Grail*, therefore, actually represent earlier versions: Erec becomes Geraint, Yvain is called Owein, and the hero of the Grail story, Perceval, is replaced by Peredur, while all of the stories are cast in a more primitive mould.

Elsewhere in the same collection we find Arthur displaying further Celtic attributes. In the story of *Culhwch and Olwen* we are given a glimpse of an Arthurian court probably not far removed from the sixth-century one – although Arthur has already become a 'king' and his warriors are more than slightly touched with the magical abilities of myth and legend. An astonishing list of heroes numbers over 250, many of whom possess attributes of a different kind to those one might expect to find among the putative 'Knights of the Round Table'.[62] There were, for example:

> Gila Stag Shank, who could leap three hundred acres in a single bound ... Gweveyl son of Gwastad (when he was sad he would let one lid droop to his navel and raise the other until it was a hood over his head), ... Gwrhyr Interpreter of Tongues, who knew all

> tongues . . . Cust son of Clustveinydd (were he buried seven fathoms
> in the earth he would hear an ant stirring from its bed fifty miles
> away).
>
> (trans. J. Gantz.)

Thus the magnetic figure of Arthur drew to him a vast panoply of
Celtic heroes, whose honour it became to serve at his court. Of
many of them we now know nothing more than their names; yet
some are familiar. Kai (the later Sir Kay), Bedwyr (better known
as Sir Bedivere), and Owein (the Sir Ywain of French and English
romances) are there among the fantastic cavalcade of Otherwordly
characters, while Arthur himself remains the outstanding figure,
cloaked in the majesty and mystery of the Celtic world.

In *Culhwch and Olwen* for example he must always give gifts
when asked for in a certain way – though he may occasionally
make exceptions:

> you shall have the request that head and tongue name . . . excepting
> only my ship, my mantle, my sword Caledvwich, my spear Rhongo-
> mynyad, my shield Wynebgwrthucher, my knife Carnwennan and my
> wife Gwenhwyvar.
>
> (trans. J. Gantz.)

This list of Otherworld weaponry shows that Arthur himself had
by this stage acquired Otherwordly origins or that he had 'stolen'
them. Evidence of this is to be found in an early Welsh poem called
Preiddeu Annwn,[45] *The Spoils (i.e. treasure) of Annwn*. In this
Arthur leads a band of warriors on a raid into the realm of the dead
to steal the Cauldron of Arawn, which could restore to life any dead
warrior placed within it.

More than just another adventure lies behind this. It is evident
that Arthur, by acquiring this trophy, also acquired for himself
something of the power of the Lord of the Otherworld. Thus we
are not surprised to find him, in another story, ordering the exhuma-
tion of the head of Bran, the great guardian spirit of Britain, on
the grounds that he alone, Arthur Pendragon, should defend the
island.

The great Celticist Jean Markale sees in these episodes indication
of a conflict between Arthur and the Lords of the Otherworld; hence
the number of magicians and enchantresses to be found visiting the
Otherworld with the object of testing both Arthur himself and all his
knights. Perhaps also we may see evidence of another inheritance,
both racial and religious, in the number of queens and Otherwordly

women who represent, in some sort, the presence of goddesses once worshipped in these islands.

The literary career of Arthur continued unabated for another 300 years, with countless new stories and retellings appearing throughout Britain and Europe. New characters appeared, or became attracted into the Arthurian ambience. Celtic warriors such as Gwalchmai and Lleminawg, traded their old names and customs for new, and as 'Gawain' and 'Lancelot' became the most widely known and written about characters in the whole of Western courtly literature.

The portraits of Arthur were not always flattering. In several early chronicles he is given the epithet *Horribilus* and described as a tyrant. In later romances he falls for a Saxon enchantress, lives for two and a half years with a twin half-sister of Guinevere who has been substituted for the real queen (this is made the excuse for Lancelot and the real Guinevere to become lovers), and generally falls into a slothful state from which more than one effort has to be made to rouse him.

Yet despite these (comparativly minor) shortcomings, Arthur remains the shining example of all that a Christian king should be. When William Caxton published his edition of Thomas Malory's *Le Morte d'Arthur* in 1485 he described in his preface how numerous people had reproached him with failing to print a history of 'the most renowned Christian King ... Arthur, which ought to be remembered among us English men to fore of all other Christian kings'.

Malory's book retold the story of Arthur from birth to death, in prose which has seldom been equalled. It was a threnody for the dying age of chivalry, which Arthur and his knights above all represented. It has ensured that the stories of the noble Fellowship of the Round Table have not been forgotten, and that the tradition they embody has remained evergreen.

THE MYTHIC HERO

Far more than the memory of a great and heroic leader was being recorded here. More ancient memories were stirred to life by the deeds of the historical Arthur than were recorded in the romances or the pseudo-histories. Beneath these, as beneath the level of the Celtic stories, existed a further dimension – an older, deeper set of mythically conceived archetypes, which became forged by time and circumstance into a cycle which has stood the test of the ages and continues to affect anyone who encounters it.

From time to time we catch a glimpse of these mighty figures behind the patina of Celtic or medieval legends, as in the story of *The Dream of Rhonabwy*, from the *Mabinogion*. Here, Rhonabwy, who may well have lived in thirteenth-century Wales, falls asleep on a magical ox's hide which induces in him a dream of the mythical past. He sees himself and his companions riding across a plain, where they encounter first of all Iddawg, son of Mynyo, who is described as follows:

> he saw a young man with curly hair and a newly trimmed beard riding a yellow horse. This man was green from the tops of his legs and his kneecaps down, and wore a tunic of yellow brocade sewn with green thread; on his thigh was a gold-hilted sword, with a scabbard of new cordovan and a gold buckle. Over the tunic he wore a mantle of yellow brocade sewn with green silk, and the green of the rider's outfit and his horse's was the colour of fir needles, while the yellow was the colour of broom. His bearing was so awesome that they became frightened and fled, but he gave chase; when his horse breathed out they drew ahead, but when it breathed in they were as near as its chest.
>
> (trans. J. Gantz.)

If we were in any doubt that this represents the first stage of a fully fledged mythic scenario, this is confirmed by the remainder of the story, as Rhonabwy and his companions meet successive members of Arthur's war-band and finally the king himself. When Iddawg presents Rhonabwy, Arthur's reaction is first to ask where he found these 'little men', and then to bemoan the fate of the land for 'being in the care of such puny men ... after the sort that held it before' (*ibid.*).

All great heroes may seen like giants to the mortal who enters the Otherworld, but this is because they are mythic archetypes, drawn from the deepest levels of the human imagination.

We find further indication of this a little later in the same text, where Arthur and his nephew Owein play a game of *gwyddbwyll*, which is akin to chess and possesses profound symbolic qualities. While they are playing, a battle begins between Owein's 'ravens' and Arthur's men, and a succession of messengers appears to report increasing degrees of carnage on both sides. Each time, either Arthur or Owein request the withdrawal of their forces, and each time the response is the ritualised formula 'Play on', until at last Arthur's anger is such that he crushes the game pieces to golden dust, whereat the combat ceases as abruptly as it had begun.

This strange contest has many levels of meaning. Owein's ravens are really Otherwordly women who possess the ability to transform their shape; they are the sisters of Owein's mother or aunt, the goddess Modron, who conforms both to the archetype of the Great Mother and to that of Sovereignty, the tutelary goddess of the land – so that at another level the battle between Arthur and his nephew is for the rulership, the sovereignty of the inner land of Britain. It is, perhaps, an annual event, which continues to take place in the Otherworld even though Arthur has himself long been withdrawn from the world of men.

For the King is also, like all great mythic heroes, deathless. At the end of his earthly career, after the great battle at Camlan (site unknown) in which he fights against his own son, Mordred, he receives a wound beyond the skills of mortal healing. But there comes the enchantress Morgan le Fay, Arthur's half-sister, who until that moment had been his implacable enemy, and after searching the wound she takes him away, in her magical boat, to Avalon, the island paradise of the Celts, to be healed and to await a future call to his country's need.

Thus Arthur conforms in every detail to the mythic archetype. Strangely born, his end is mysterious. His relationship with the Goddess of the land and her avatars is established early. He summons a great fellowship of heroes to sit at his circular table which echoes, as Merlin says, 'the roundness of the world', and also the circle of the heavens. He is placed in polarised balance by the presence of Morgan, who acts always against him until the end, then appears as his guardian and protectress. He possesses magical weapons – in particular, of course, Excalibur, which must be returned to the lake when he no longer requires it. With his going the world is a lesser place; though his dream, of a unified, perfected earthly kingdom, remains, to be taken up and renewed throughout time to our own days, and doubtless beyond.

In the great romances, which added successive dimensions to Arthur's career, drawing in the great cycle of the Grail, and annexing the adventures of many individual heroes until these formed a constellation around the central star that was Arthur, we may see a dream being worked out. It is not simply Merlin's dream of a unified, earthly kingdom expressing the highest values known to man; it is the encapsulated desire of an age that even in its most violent moments consistently sought to reach upward to heaven and touch the hand of God. It is, in the end, an expression of all that is best in what Sir Galahad, in Thomas Malory's great book, called 'this unstable world'.

That it continues to stand for these things is all the indication we should need as to its validity and extraordinary power.

EXERCISE 1: THE STARRY KING

This exercise is designed to establish contact with the inner reality behind the myth of Arthur. From this beginning will spring many things as you continue to explore the age-old mysteries of the Arthurian Tradition.

Close your eyes and imagine that you are standing at the summit of a high hill. It is night and all around you are the noises of the night: the bark of a fox, the shrill screech of an owl. But more than this, the air itself is filled with an energy which resonates within you like an audible note. You look up and see that the sky is filled with stars, which shine so clearly that you feel you can almost reach up and touch them. As you look your attention is drawn to one particular quarter of the heavens: the north. There you perceive a pattern of stars which you had not noticed before. They form a rough circle, through which a patch of sky shows that is empty. As you look the circle seems to grow larger, to get nearer, until you are looking into what seems like a window in the heavens.

Into this now comes a scattering of new stars which take up the shape of a crowned figure, outlined in light. This is the Starry King, who stands always behind the archetype of Arthur. A great hand and arm of light reaches down, and you feel yourself lifted up, cupped as in a mighty palm, and set down again, on an island of cloud. Beneath your feet the ground is firm, and you walk a little way until you see before you a low green mound on which grows a clump of trees. There, seated beneath the shade of the great boughs, is the king, chin in hand, staring out at something which as yet remains hidden to you. As you approach he turns, and you see in his eyes many things reflected – the starry sky, your own face, and something more, an understanding and recognition of your own destiny. You have a chance to speak with him if you wish, or you may simply sit for a while in silence, sharing his vigil until it is time for you to depart . . .

You will know when the moment comes to leave, and will take your leave of the king accordingly. Before you depart he offers you a blessing, which is yours to accept or refuse as you wish. If you choose to accept it you may be sure that its effects will be felt in your life for many weeks or months to come.

Turning, you walk away from the island across the cloudy floor, and feel yourself once again gently lifted up, carried and set down in the place from which you began. The circle of stars grows smaller and more distant and you become aware again of the night sky and the hilltop where you stand. Then this too slowly fades and you become aware again of your normal surroundings. Open your eyes and re-establish contact with the outer world.

2 · MERLIN AND THE PROPHECIES OF THE LAND:

VISION AND ENCHANTMENT AT CAMELOT

And those who knew Merlin well and who had served Uther Pendragon came to the king and said to him: 'Sire, honour Merlin greatly for he was a good prophet for your father and has always loved your family much. And he foretold to Vertiger his death and it was he who had the Round Table made. Now see to it that he is well honoured, for you will never ask him about anything that he will not tell you.' And Arthur responded that thus he would do.

Didot Perceval

GOD OR DRUID?

Nowhere is the inner nature of the Arthurian Tradition more clearly focused than in the figure of Merlin. Adviser to three kings, prophet, magician and wise man, his shadowy presence seldom takes any single form for long enough to observe his real nature. His genesis, within the 'Matter of Britain', is almost as complex.

One commentator has called him a god of the ancient, native people of Britain; his home, at Maridunum, was also the site of his cult.[2] Others have seen in him a shaman or a wild man,[83] an inner guardian of the land [32] or a seer whose prophecies have a very real validity for our own time.[78] But he eludes any fixed definitions; his origins and his ultimate fate remain as mysterious as at the time of his first appearance. Even his own words render him more opaque: 'Because I am dark, and always shall be, let my book be dark and mysterious in those places where I will not show myself.[70]

Some aspects of his career we can point to, however. He first appears in recognisable form in the writings of the twelfth-century pseudo-historian Geoffrey of Monmouth who may have heard stories of Merlin either during his childhood in Monmouth or in his later days as Bishop of St Asaph in North Wales. Either way Merlin plays a considerable role in his *History of the Kings of Britain*, and he also wrote (or compiled) a volume of Merlin's prophecies, which he incorporated into his larger work as part of the history of early Britain.

The veracity of Geoffrey's book has been the cause of scholarly debate for generations, and while many earlier critics dismissed him as a flagrant forger, a more recent attitude tends to emphasis his value as a recorder of traditional tales and native folklore. R.J. Stewart, in his valuable study of the Prophecies,[78] has established that Geoffrey must have had access to a large collection of material which recorded Merlin's inspired utterances – although whether these were entirely genuine, or represented a Merlin tradition, has yet to be completely established.

The story of the occasion of Merlin's great prophetic outburst, as told by Geoffrey, deserves to be detailed in full. Vortigern, a minor king, makes a bid for power by bringing in Saxon mercenaries to fight the Picts in the north and his own enemies elsewhere. He is briefly popular, but his star soon wanes as more and more Saxons arrive and begin acquiring larger and larger areas of land. Finally the exiled sons of the former High King of Britain return at the head of an army and Vortigern flees to Wales, where he intends to build a stronghold. Having chosen a site, he sets his builders to work; but every night the progress they have made is undone by a mysterious agency. Vortigern consults his druids and learns that only the blood of a fatherless child, spilled on the stones, will ensure the completion of the fortress. Sent out to search for such a child, Vortigern's soldiers discover Merlin at

Carmarthen (said by Geoffrey to derive from *Caer Myrddin*, Merlin's Town). He is the son of a Welsh princess, but no one knows his father. The woman and her son are brought before Vortigern, and Merlin's mother explains that she has led a devout and pure life, but that she was visited in her chamber by a golden being who fathered the child upon her. Vortigern is tempted to disbelieve this account, but Merlin himself speaks out in defence of his mother, and challenges Vortigern and his druids to explain the real reason why the tower will not stand. He tells them that there is a pool beneath the hilltop, and that within it is a stone coffer containing two dragons, one red and the other white, who battle mightily every night, thus causing the ground to shake and the work of the king's masons to fall. Vortigern orders his men to dig and finds that all is as Merlin had foretold. The wise child then explains that the red dragon symbolises Britain and the white dragon the Saxons, and prophesies that after a time the white will overcome the red. He then goes into a trance and for the extent of the next twelve to fourteen pages in Geoffrey's book proceeds to expound the future of the race unto the very end of time. In the process he prophesies the coming of Arthur, 'the Boar of Cornwall', which will 'bring relief from these invaders, for it will trample their necks beneath its feet', and warns Vortigern of his own forthcoming death. The end of this extraordinary outburst is apocalyptic, with references to riot among the planetary houses and the fall of deadly rain. Finally,

> In the twinkling of an eye the seas shall rise up and the arena of the winds shall be opened once again. The Winds shall do battle together with a blast of ill-omen, making their din reverberate from one constellation to another.
>
> (trans. L. Thorpe.)

The whole structure and content of these prophecies shows a remarkable grasp of the inner tides which control the fate of the world, and Merlin's vision of the future is as terrifying as anything foretold by Nostradamus or his ilk. Wherever Geoffrey found the material for this part of his book, it was clearly not from his own mind, indicating, as already stated, that he was in some way the recipient of a body of traditional lore associated with Merlin.[77]

Geoffrey himself, as we have seen, claimed that he was merely translating 'a certain very ancient book written in the British language', lent to him by Archdeacon Walter of Oxford, and that this was the source of all that he wrote. No trace of this book has ever come to light, and it has generally been considered to be an invention by Geoffrey to add veracity to his fanciful history. However, while there seems no reason why there should not have been such a book, it is evident that Geoffrey embellished his sources considerably. It is known that the source of the story related above is the writings of the sixth-century monk, Nennius, and these are possibly one of the few authentic records of the Arthurian era. His youthful prophet was named Ambrosius, and it seems that in order not to confuse him with Ambrosius the son of Constantine, who overthrows Vortigern, Geoffrey borrowed the name of Merlin from an earlier, native figure, Merddyn Wyllt 'the Wild', who may actually have lived either in Scotland or in Wales during the sixth or seventh century.[83]

This makes him, of course, roughly contemporary with Arthur, and it is possible that we have here a genuine tradition of the great war-leader and his inspired advisor which has been carried through to reappear in Geoffrey's text in a mangled form.

Whatever the truth of the matter, it was to have a profound effect on the history of Merlin. Geoffrey's book, as we have seen, became a best-seller throughout the Middle Ages, and may well have given the initial impetus to the entire phenomenon of Arthurian literature. After the episode of Vortigern's tower and his first great prophetic outpouring, Merlin went on to perform several prodigious feats – including the moving of a ring of magical stones called 'The Giant's Dance' from Ireland to Salisbury Plain, where they became a vast mausoleum for the Kings of Britain (better known as Stonehenge).

While Merlin was clearly not responsible for the building of the great megalithic monument, it is possible that even here Geoffrey was recording an ancient tradition which related to the original builders of the great stone circle.[75] He went on to serve both the sons of King Constantine, Ambrosius Aurelianus and Uther Pendragon, who became the father of Arthur, and it is to Geoffrey again that we owe the famous story of the hero's conception, in which Merlin magically disguises Uther to look like the husband of the Duchess of Cornwall so that he can lie with her and beget the future king.

Subsequently Merlin becomes adviser to Arthur, in which guise he is still best remembered, and as which he appears in all the major versions of the story which follow Geoffrey's account. He thus serves three kings, for each of whom he performs remarkable feats, while serving as prophet and adviser. He is never pictured as a mere court magician however; there is always something restless and untamable about him, vestiges of a wild and Otherworldly dimension continue to cling to him, and for this also we owe something to Geoffrey of Monmouth.

THE LIFE OF MERLIN

For Geoffrey was not finished with the character of Merlin. He wrote another book, in Latin verse, called the *Vita Merlini, The Life of Merlin*[77] in which he extended his account of the famous prophet to an even greater degree. Here he paints a very different picture from that of his earlier works. Merlin is a prince in his own right who, driven mad by the scenes of carnage at the battle of Arderydd, run away and lives like a wild beast in the wilderness for many years before returning at last to sanity and becoming recognised as a great prophet and wise man.

In this Geoffrey was drawing again on the traditions surrounding the mysterious figure of Myrddin Wyllt, who seems to have lived in

Merlin by Aubrey Beardsley

17

post-Arthurian Britain and to have absorbed something of an even earlier, possibly deified being of great antiquity. Some of the writings of this historical Myrddin have actually survived, and show him to have been no mean poet.

APPLE TREES

Sweet appletree that luxuriantly grows!
Food I used to take at its base to please a fair maid,
When, with my shield on my shoulder, and my sword on
my thigh,
I slept all alone in the woods of Celyddon.

Hear, O little pig! now apply thyself to reason,
And listen to birds whose notes are pleasant,
Sovereigns across the sea will come on Monday;
Blessed will the Cymry [Welsh] be from that design.
Sweet appletree, which grows by the riverside!
With respect to it, the keeper will not thrive on its splendid
fruit.
While my reason was not aberrant, I used to be around its
stem
With a fair sportive maid, a paragon of splendid form.
Ten years and forty, as the toy of lawless ones,
Have I been wandering in gloom and among sprites . . .

Sweet appletree, and a tree of crimson hue,
Which grew in concealment in the wood of Celyddon;
They sought for their fruit, it will be in vain,
Until Cadwaladyr comes from the conference of Rhyd
Rheon,
And Cynon to meet him advances upon the Saxons;
The Cymry will be victorious, glorious will be their leader.
All shall have their rights, and the Brython will rejoice,
Sounding the horns of gladness, and chanting the song of
peace and happiness!
(trans. W.F. Skene, *Four Ancient Books of Wales*.)

This is full of curious lore and the remains of the tradition which depicts Myrddin living wild among the woods with only a pig for company (the pig was regarded as a sacred beast among the Celts). It shows that, whatever else he may have been, Merlin (or Myrddin) was very much a part of the ancient bardic tradition of Wales. Together with those of Taliesin, Aneurin, and Llwyarch Hen, his writings form part of a significant body of literature which has survived (not without a good deal of reworking) to the present day. I have elsewhere undertaken a study of this tradition,[59] which proves to contain the last vestiges of native British shamanism. Although it is of a different tone to the accounts of Merlin's later career, many of his magical acts are duplicated in this more primitive strain of material.

By drawing together these elusive threads of tradition Geoffrey provided a foundation on which many generations of writers could build. The wonder-working prophet of the *Historia* and the *Vita* proved immensely popular with the medieval audiences – as, indeed, he has continued to be. Numerous texts followed, which extended his role even further, until he became a central figure within Arthurian tradition.

THE DEVIL'S SON

Inevitably perhaps, in one so talented in the reading of the stars and the future, Merlin became associated in the medieval consciousness with the idea of necromancy, and thus with the devil. When the twelfth-century Burgundian writer Robert de Borron, as he had previously done with the Grail legends (see Chapter 6), set about filling in some of the details of Merlin's history missing from the earlier records, he gave a very different account.

He described the demons of Hell, infuriated by Christ's descent and purgation of their overcrowded domain, plotting the birth of an anti-Christ – Merlin. They sent forth a minor demon of the kind known as a *succubus*, who was to overshadow an innocent Princess of Dyfed and father upon her a child of evil. Their plans are frustrated by the innate goodness of the child's mother, who finds a priest to baptise the infant before evil can take hold of him. He is born with a hairy pelt and the ability to speak and reason almost from birth. The hair falls from him when he is baptized, but he retains both the power of speech and an Otherworldly clairvoyance.

Thus Merlin's abilities are accounted for in terms acceptable to a Christian readership; the 'golden stranger' of the earlier tales becomes a demon, the 'god' a 'devil', and powers which would have been wholly appropriate to a Celtic god become magical and wondrous – the product of necromancy. Their effects remain the same, however; Merlin as magician reigns supreme.

Interestingly, Merlin's mother is described as a Princess of Dyfed, and in Geoffrey's *Vita Merlini*, we may remember, he is also described as a prince in his own right. This seems to add yet one more strand to the complex web of associations. No record of a sixth-century noble named Merlin or Myrddin has come to light, but this does not mean that no such person existed. The overlay of mythical and historical figures is anyway so complete that it is no longer possible to differentiate one from the other.

In the same way, Merlin the prophet seems to have assumed some of the attributes and abilities of an inspired semi-mythical madman named Lailoken, who hailed from the Lowlands of Scotland at roughly the same period as Merlin may have flourished. Through this character Merlin derives certain aspects of the Scottish St Kentigern, whose history reflects that of the mage at several points, and who was instrumental in restoring Lailoken to sanity.

A story common to both Merlin and Lailoken concerns their laughter: in each instance they laugh three times at unlikely events, betraying their uncanny knowledge by so doing. Merlin laughs at the wife of his friend King Rhydderch when he sees a leaf caught in her hair – the heritage of an adulterous tryst; again at a beggar whom he knows to be sitting over a pot of gold; and a third time at a youth buying a new pair of shoes when in fact he is destined to die within the day.

The theme is an old one and derives ultimately from Oriental sources – as indeed do several other aspects of Merlin's career, prompting one commentator to suggest that his origins may have been further east than we have come to suspect.[19] However, this only serves to show how closly Merlin came to conform to the image of the magician. In common with two other poets, the Celtic Taliesin and the Roman Virgil, his demonstrable knowledge of other levels of meaning and understanding caused the aspect of the magician to be grafted upon him. The prophetic element derived from Lailoken, or from more ancient records, and the final image became that of the wise magician and counsellor of Arthur's court.

Additional to this is the idea of Merlin's shamanic background. Several traces of this remain, in his ability to change shape at will (particularly into the form of a stag, a typical shamanic totem beast), his prophetic and inspired utterances, and the motif of the threefold death, identified by R.J. Stewart in his two books about Merlin.[77,78]

Here, Merlin's sister Ganeida, to test his newly restored sanity, presents him with the same youth in three different guises. In each case Merlin predicts a different end for the youth, who will hang, drown and fall to his death. This prediction is fulfilled when the youth falls over a cliff, and is suspended by an ankle caught in a tree root with his head beneath the waters of a river.

In the story of mad Lailoken the prophet predicts the threefold death for himself, from which we may justly believe that the same thing once held good for Merlin also. The motif is an extremely ancient one, deriving ultimately from the self-initiation, or false-death of the shaman. It reappears in esoteric symbolism in the tarot card of 'The Hanged Man', and signifies the relationship of the magician/shaman to the elements.

Although we are able to delineate these aspects of Merlin separately, the overall portrait remains consistent, suggesting a single figure behind the projected aspects. Even the manner of his departure from the world bears an overall similarity despite surface differences.

MERLIN AND NIMUE

The reference to 'a fair, sportive maid' in the poem quoted above may indicate the antiquity of a final theme. This is Merlin's fatal love for the fairy Nimue, sometimes called Niniane or Vivienne, who is pictured as having stolen his power and used it to bind him, still living, for all time.

We first hear of Nimue in the Merlin section of the vast Arthurian compilation known as *The Vulgate Cycle*.[71] This massive collection of story and polemic was written down during the first half of the thirteenth century, by clerks belonging to the order of Cistercian monks, founded by the great medieval theologian Bernard of Clairvaux. While specifically Christianising the material, it also drew upon a vast range of earlier works, including one which gave a more complex rendition of Robert de Borron's *Merlin*.

Here we read of the forester Dionas, so named because of his devotion to the Goddess Diana, who had a daughter named Niniane, of whom the Goddess spoke the following prophecy:

> I grant thee, and so doth the god of the sea and the stars . . . that the first female child that thou shalt have shall be much coveted by the wisest man that ever was on earth . . . and he shall teach her the most part of his wit and cunning by way of necromancy, in such manner that he shall be so desirous after he hath seen her, that he shall have no power to do nothing against her wish, and all things that she enquireth he shall teach.
>
> (From the Middle English version, slightly modernised by the author).

21

Niniane is thus in some sense regarded as under the aegis of the goddess, just as her father is described as her 'god-son' a euphemistic way of saying that he was a worshipper of Diana. As to the prophecy, it is proved to be accurate in the story which follows, given here in the version of Malory.

> Merlin fell in a dotage on one of the damosels of the lake, that hight Nimue. But Merlin would let her have no rest, but always he would be with her. And ever she made Merlin good cheer till she had learned of him all manner of thing that she desired; and he was assotted upon her . . . and always . . . lay about the lady to have her maidenhood, and she was ever passing weary of him, and fain would have been delivered of him because he was a devil's son . . . And so on a time it happened that Merlin showed her a rock whereat was a great wonder . . . So by her subtle working she made Merlin to go under that stone . . . but she wrought . . . for him that he came never out for all the craft that he could do. And so she departed and left Merlin.
>
> (Bk IV, Ch. 1.)

This somewhat unflattering portrayal of the aged Merlin, besotted on the beautiful fairy damsel (one of the Ladies of the Lake no less!) who cozens his secrets out of him and then uses them to imprison him, seems to be part of the general tendency on the part of certain medieval writers to seek a Christian interpretation of often quite primitive pagan material. Thus Merlin himself becomes the son of a devil, rather than an Otherworldly being, and Nimue, whose father served the goddess Diana, is portrayed as a temptress whose power derives solely from that of Merlin.

The *Vita Merlini* portrays Merlin as having a sister, Ganeida, whose own wisdom is no less than his. When the moment comes for him to retire from the world, as it does to all high initiates, Merlin withdraws along with Ganeida, to a wonderful observatory with seventy-two windows, from which they observe the stars and hold lengthy philosophical discussions upon the meaning of creation. Perhaps we may look to this story for the origin of Nimue, transformed from sister to temptress, who thus has to extract the wisdom of Merlin by the use of her wiles. Even the portrayal of Merlin as an old man stems from a misconception – nowhere is his age specifically stated, and he does, in fact, take the forms both of an old man and of a youth on more than one occasion.

Neither is it without significance that the last person to hear the voice of Merlin is another character who underwent similiar down-grading within the works of predominantly Christian interpreters. This was Gawain who, as I have shown elsewhere, began life as the Champion of the Goddess and ended it as a murderer and a libertine.[59] Thus it seems wholly appropriate that, happening to pass by the great stone under which the mage is imprisoned, it is Gawain who hears 'the cry of Merlin'.

Afterwards Merlin's tomb becomes known as the *Perron de Merlin* or Stone of Merlin and there the knights of the Round Table meet to begin their adventures. Thus even in his withdrawn state Merlin may be said to influence the doings of the Arthurian world, and indeed the seeds he had planted in the early days of Arthur's reign are meant to prepare the way for the great Quest for the Holy Grail – though this was not to begin for many years after his departure.

Significantly, apropos of this, in another version Merlin remarks that he must withdraw because: 'Those who are gathered together here must believe what they see happen and I would not that they should think that I had brought it about.'[70] Then, as now, the words of the *withdrawn* prophet meant more than those of the teacher in the flesh.

The most mysterious version of Merlin's departure is that which describes him as retreating into an *esplumoir*, a word which has no precise meaning but which is sometimes interpreted as referring to a 'moulting cage' in which hawks are placed to shed their feathers. Symbolically this seems clear enough: Merlin withdraws to shed the form of his current life and to adopt a new spiritual garment. From within his moulting cage he is enabled to see far more then ever before, and his influence extends further, beyond the confines of the Arthurian Kingdom into the world at large. He remains, as the psychologist Carl Jung called him, 'the age-old son of the mother'[86], able to perceive the greatest depths and to work within the inner realms towards the integration of mankind with deity – the final aim of all such co-workers with god.

Thus we may see that Merlin conforms at every level to their image of the inner master, the great soul who is able to participate at will in the outer history of creation. His presence alone lifts the Arthurian tradition above that of many similiar sagas. In the next chapters we shall examine further how this inner dimension impinges continually on the outer working of the stories.

EXERCISE 2: MERLIN'S TOWER

You are standing on a green trackway that winds between fields of blue cornflowers. Before you a little way ahead is a tall, narrow tower, reaching upwards into the clear mid-morning air. As you approach it you see that it has several narrow windows indicating five floors, and a wooden door, closed at present, with a curious brass knocker made up of entwined serpents. On the door is written: *The Wisdom of the Heart*.

You raise the knocker and knock thrice, at which it opens of its own accord, revealing a flight of worn stone steps leading upwards. As you climb, counting the steps, you begin to feel a change in your metabolism: your breathing slows, your pulses beat to a strong, steady rhythm, your sight grows clearer – so that, although the tower is dark within, you have no difficulty in finding your way.

Soon you emerge on the first floor, and find yourself in a circular room in which the only furniture is a large mirror in an ornate, carved frame. A second flight of stairs leads on upwards. You may choose whether or not to go and look in the mirror, which may show you either your true self or an event from your past or future life. If you choose not to, or after you have spent some time in front of the mirror, you begin to climb upwards again, feeling as you do so, a deepening sense of awareness, so that the stones against which your hands brush as you climb seem to possess a living quality, as does the very air you breathe, which is far clearer than you would expect within the confines of the tower.

Soon you emerge on the second floor, and find yourself in a room identical to the first, save that around the walls are hung a series of tapestries depicting scenes which have a deep personal meaning for you. They may once again be events from your own life, past or future, or they may be images of archetypal importance, containing meanings not only for you but of a wider significance. You may, as before, choose whether to examine them in detail, or you may continue your ascent at once by the stair which leads on upwards.

As you climb onwards you once again experience change, this time to the sense of hearing. Tiny sounds – mice in the stonework, spiders spinning their intricate webs, birds singing outside the tower – become clear and sharp as crystal. At the very edge of hearing are voices, singing music of unearthly beauty.

Then you arrive at the third level, finding yourself this time in a room filled with light which comes from a great globe of crystal at the centre. You may approach and look within if you desire, and there you may see the ways in which your own deepest wishes are fulfilled. And this may be hard, for not all things desired happen as we might wish. If you do not wish to look within the globe, begin your ascent to the next level. If you choose to look, proceed then up the next flight of stairs.

This time the change within you is more subtle: you begin to be aware of connections, of the links which form between many different and variant things. Ideas or images, which seemed to exist independently of one another, now are seen to resonate, forming fresh thoughts or pictures.

Now, as you arrive at the fourth level, you find yourself emerging into a place where the walls are transparent, like glass or crystal, and where the winds somehow blow through them, bringing scents of the outer world – all the rich and delicate aromas of nature. You can see, with your enhanced sight, much further than you would normally be able to see, and you look out across a landscape of richness and variety. Here are mountains and valleys, rivers and streams, forests and green hillsides, wild, uncultivated lands and the colourful quilt of fields and gardens. Houses, too, you can see, with smoke curling lazily into a blue sky. If this seems to you the landscape of the Otherworld, or of an earthly paradise, you are not far from the truth, for this is Logres, the inner Kingdom of Britain, over which the great king, Arthur, once ruled.

When you have looked your fill, and have drunk of the wine of the air, you begin your ascent to the fifth and final level, this time emerging into a pleasant, airy room lined with bookshelves and with a clutter of curious objects scattered about. In a chair before a roaring fire sits a figure in robes of deep blue. His hair is white yet his face seems ever young and his eyes see deeply into you. This is Merlin, the ageless son of the Mother, whose tower you have entered and climbed. He smiles in welcome and you may if you desire approach and talk with him on any matter that concerns or puzzles you. Nothing you say will seem either too strange or too shocking to Merlin, for he has read the very books of the stars and all potential things are known to him. If you have no question or matter to discuss, you may choose to sit with him in silence for a time, until you are ready to leave.

When that time comes Merlin rises and offers you a goblet of silver in which is a clear drink. You may choose whether or not to accept this, but be sure that if you do you are imbibing truth itself, and a distillation of Merlin's wisdom which will remain yours for as long as you are worthy of it. This done, Merlin draws aside a curtain to reveal a small wooden door in the wall. He opens it for you and ushers you through . . . and you find that you have returned once more to the place from which you began your journey. Take a moment to re-establish contact with your physical surroundings then open your eyes. You will find that your senses remain enhanced for some time to come, and whatever you discussed with Merlin, or whatever thing you learned during your time within his tower will be yours to refer to whenever you have need.

3 · THE ROUND TABLE:

ADVENTURE IN THE FOREST
OF THE MIND

Arthur never heard speak of a knight in praise, but he caused him to
be numbered of his household ... Because of these noble lords
about his hall, of whom each knight pained himself to be the hardiest
champion, and none would count him the least praiseworthy, Arthur
made the Round Table ... It was ordained of Arthur that when his fair
fellowship sat to meat their chairs should be high alike, their service
equal, and none before or after his comrade. Thus no man could boast
that he was exalted above his fellow, for all alike were gathered round
the board, and none was alien at the breaking of Arthur's bread.

(Wace, *Roman de Brut*)

A TABLE IN THE LIKENESS OF THE WORLD

Once the wars that attended Arthur's ascent to the throne were over,
he decided to take a wife, and despite Merlin's warnings that she

27

would one day betray him, he selected Guinevere, the daughter of King Leodegrance of Cameliarde. With her came, as dowry, a great Round Table, made by Merlin at the bidding of Arthur's father, Uther Pendragon. A table 'round in the likeness of the world', at which one hundred and fifty knights could sit, and none seem higher in favour than the rest. And on the day of his marriage Arthur required of Merlin that he should find sufficient knights 'which be of most prowess and worship' to fill at least fifty of the seats.[47]

This Merlin did, and fifty more came from Leodegrance, so that a hundred sat down together at the table on that first day. And when they had all done homage to Arthur they returned to the hall where the Round Table stood and found that on the back of each chair was a name, set there in golden letters. The names were all of those already chosen, and many more that were as yet not come. But two remained blank, and of these Merlin would only say that they would be filled in due course.

Thus the Fellowship of the Round Table met for the first time on the day of the King's wedding to Guinevere; and if the seeds were thus already sown for the downfall of Arthur's great dream, the shadows were still distant on that day. For thus began the greatest ideal of chivalry ever to be known, the fame of which would resound through the ages, inspiring kings of many countries to emulate Arthur, and to found Orders of their own in the likeness of the Round Table.

Their first adventure followed swiftly, for as they sat at dinner there came into the hall a white hart, pursued by a white dog and fifty couples of black hounds. As they raced around the Table the white dog bit the hart, which leapt high in the air, knocking over a knight who sat to one side. This man seized the dog and departed hurriedly, and in the next moment a lady rode into the hall and demanded that he be brought back, for the dog was hers. But before anyone could answer, a fully armed knight rode among them, and seizing the lady carried her off by force.

Astonishment, and perhaps some amusement, attended these events. But Merlin stood forth and stated that the Fellowship 'might not leave these adventures so lightly', and so Arthur sent two of the new knights – his own nephew, Sir Gawain, and the illegitimate son of King Pellinore, Sir Tor – out after the white hart and the dog respectively; and Pellinore himself, a tried and trusted warrior, after the lady who had been stolen away.

So at the outset this single incident had given rise to three separate adventures, which are there and then narrated at length. They are to be the first of many such which begin in similar fashion, with the

The Round Table in the Great Hall in Winchester Castle

entry of knight or lady into the court, requesting succour or some favour of Arthur and of the Fellowship. Nor may they refuse, so long as the request is a fair one, and the demand honest. For at the end of that first, triple quest, all of the Fellowship swears on oath:

> Never to do outrage nor murder, and always to flee treason; also, by no means to be cruel, but to give mercy unto him that asketh mercy, upon pain of forfeiture of their worship and lordship of King Arthur for evermore; and always to do ladies, damosels, and gentlewomen succour, upon pain of death. Also, that no man take no battles in a wrongful quarrell for no law, nor for world's goods. Unto this were all the knights sworn of the Table Round, both old and young. And every year were they sworn at the high feast of Pentecost.[47]

The rules are simply stated. They depend very much on the understood, but seldom phrased, ideals of medieval chivalry. Being human, not all of the knights keep to these demands placed upon them by their King. But despite some failings, they hold true to the honour of the Round Table, and as if in answer to their existence strange events seem to multiply on every side, seeing to it that they never lack the opportunity of being tested and tried.

Arthur establishes a custom, whereby at any high feast he will not eat until some wonder or adventure has been related to him. And so begins a pattern, whereby the knights ride 'at errantry', wandering hither and thither throughout the land in search of wrongs to right or villainy to combat. Brother knights are rescued, as well as ladies; evil knights are overthrown, and either killed or sent to Arthur to crave pardon. Many of these become Round Table Knights themselves, giving up their former pursuits. But there are always others, always further adventures to attempt, as the great knights on their great horses thunder through the forests of Arthur's realm in quest of their King's dream of chivalry and the perfect earthly kingdom.

THE FOREST AND THE LANDS ADVENTUROUS

Most of the adventures of the Round Table Fellowship seem to take place in the setting of deep, primaeval forest. This in part reflects the physical appearance of the countryside at the time when most of the romances were written; but there is a deeper significance than this. The forest symbolised an untamed world, where almost anything could, and did, lie in wait for the unwary. It stood, also, for a certain state of mind, a place to be reached on the long road from birth to death – Dante's impenetrable forest of the mind in which the soul, wakening as he expressed it 'midway through life's journey', found itself with a thousand possible ways through the darkness of the world beneath the trees.[11]

The forest, too, was part of the Otherworld, a vast uncharted tract which lay along the borders between the world of Middle Earth and the realms of Faery. Certain parts were given names: Broceliande, Arden, Inglewood: dark places redolent of enchantment, where only those intent upon adventure would willingly go. Here rode Arthur himself, in pursuit of innocent sport, to be met by the terrifyingly powerful Gromer Somer Jour, whose name means Man of the Summer's Day and who could bind him at will and demand that he discover the answer to an impossible question, or face the consequences.[23]

Or on another occasion, again hunting, the queen and her escort, who happened to be on this occasion Sir Gawain, became separated from the rest of their party and found themselves sheltering near the fearful Tarn Watheling, where more than one adventure had begun. There, they witnessed a horrific apparition, the ghost of Guinevere's mother, who 'yammered' horribly at them, and warned of dread things to come.

Yet though the forest contained many terrors, it contained as many wonders. From its depths came beautiful faery women, to test and beguile the wandering knights as they plied their course through the trees. Many sought husbands among the Fellowship who sired sons upon them – introducing a strain of Otherworldly blood into the company.

One such was Sir Launfal, who wandered into the Otherworld, met and married a beautiful fée, and was sworn to secrecy on pain of losing his love forever. Yet he was unable to keep silent when Queen Guinevere herself approached him with words of love, and in desperation he declared that even she, for all her renowned beauty, was no match for his own dear love.

Earning in this way the enmity of the queen, Launfal faced death or banishment rather than speak further, and was finally vilified by the appearance of the fée herself, who entered the court and outshone every woman there, and who then carried Launfal away with her, 'to Avalon, it is believed'.[48]

Not all such women encountered in the forest were as fair of face and speech. Ragnall, one of many archetypes of the sovereignty-bestowing goddess of the land, appeared as a hideous, Loathly Lady, who tricks Arthur into promising her the person of Sir Gawain in marriage in return for a favour. Her subsequent appearance at court, her gross manners and appearance, perhaps in part prepare one for her transformation, which occurs on the wedding night, when Ragnall, who has been 'enchanted', is restored to her true beauty through Gawain's love and understanding.

Elsewhere in the depths of the forest roamed the Questing Beast, a creature part lion, part serpent, part goat, which made a sound as though thirty couples of hounds were in its belly. Arthur first glimpses it as a youth, before he is crowned king and it presages a meeting with Merlin, who appears first as a child, then as an old man, who tells Arthur of his birth and parentage and makes many cryptic references to future events. The Beast he does not explain, but we learn that it was given birth to by a woman who had condemned a man to be torn to pieces by dogs. It exists solely to be sought after, and is followed for many years by King Pellinore. After his death the Saracen knight Palomides takes up the quest, but seems never to succeed, for this is a *ferlie*, a wonder out of the Otherworld which cannot be caught or pinned down by any mortal being.

Men and women who had the power to change themselves into animals were not infrequent in the Arthurian world. In one story Arthur follows a strange, composite beast which turns into a venerable, white-haired man;[9] in another we have one of the earliest tales concerning a werewolf, *Bisclavret*,[48] in which a knight cursed with this affliction is first betrayed by his wife and her lover, and then finally vilified and returned to his own form after many years in wolf-shape.

In the Welsh story *The Lady of the Fountain*[46] we encounter 'the Lord of the Beasts', who has one foot, one eye and one arm, who commands all the beasts of the forest, who gather about him like a congregation listening to a sermon. And when the knight Kynon asks him what power he has over the animals,

> 'I will show thee, little man', said he. And he took his club in his hand, and with it he struck a stag a great blow so that he brayed vehemently, and at his braying the animals came together, as numerous as the stars in the sky . . . and he looked at them, and bade them go and feed; and they bowed their heads, and did him homage as vassals to their lord.[46]

Other knights become attached to a specific beast: Owain to a lion;[8] Gawain to a wondrous mule,[87] or a horse which leads him into strange lands.[59] These are all, to some extent, like the totem beasts of the shaman, which act as guides to the soul in its journeys about the Otherworld.

WAR WITH THE OTHERWORLD

So many strange and wondrous beings emerge from the depths of the forest that one almost begins to wonder, after a time, if there is not some kind of struggle going on between Arthur and the denizens of the Otherworld. An early Welsh poem, the *Preiddeu Annwn* (*Spoils of the Underworld*), depicts him as leading an extraordinary band of heroes into the realm of the gods in search of a miraculous cauldron, 'Warmed by the breath of Nine Maidens'. Passing through seven levels, each one guarded by a fortress – their names are Caer Siddi, Caer Rigor, Caer Vandwy, Caer Pedryfan, Caer Goludd, and Caer Ochren – Arthur and his men steal the cauldron and return with it to the outside world. 'Except seven, none returned', the poet remarks laconically, implying that the treasure was not brought out without cost.[45]

But the realms of faery and of Arthur overlap at every point. Even in the quest for the Grail, perhaps the greatest challenge to the Fellowship, the signs and symbols of the Otherworld are threaded like a strand of silver through the scarlet tapestry of Christian miracle and dream.

In the *Lais* of Marie de France[48], composed in the twelfth century by this remarkable woman of whom virtually nothing more is known, this Otherworldliness enters in as strongly as anywhere. Marie drew for her inspiration on tales then still circulating orally in France and Brittany – tales redolent with folk lore and the magic of faery. They are Celtic wizardry in courtly dress, written for the elegant, literate audience at the court of another Marie, of Champagne, the daughter of the redoubtable Eleanor of Aquitaine, who could herself have passed for one of the gentlewomen of the Arthurian milieu.

From the Lands Adventurous, via the Black Pine, to the Fountain of Barenton, hidden deep in the Valley of No Return, the Knights of the Round Table rode 'overthwart and endlong'[47] the length and breadth of the land. Wherever the marvellous menagerie of their heraldic devices – eagles, bulls, ravens and lions – appeared, they were recognised, and their aid or company sought. Like the legendary 'fast guns' of the Old West, they were sought out by those wishing to prove themselves as the best among the chivalry of the land – maybe even earn for themselves a seat at the famous Table.

Two great families provided many of the leading figures of the cycle: those of Orkney and those of de Galles. The Orkney clan, Gawain, Gaheries, Agravain and Gareth, were the sons of King Lot of Orkney and his queen, Morgause, who was Arthur's half-sister and also the mother of the bastard Mordred. The de Galles family, Perceval, Lamorack and Aglovale, were the sons of King Pellinore (the mother is not named) who had also numerous illegitimate by-blows – including the great Sir Tor or Torre – and a legitimate daughter who is sometimes named Dindraine, and played an important part in the quest for the Grail.

There was much rivalry between these two families, sparked off by the killing of Lot by Pellinore, after which the Orkney faction, led by Gawain, carried out several murderous vengeance attacks, which led to the deaths of Morgause and Lamorack, who became lovers until Gaheries killed his own mother and the brothers together slew Lamorack.

Despite such internecine struggles, Malory referred to the Fellowship as 'the high order of Chivalry' and made of it something above average for the time, more in line with the kind of idea expressed in treatises on the subject, like that of the Spanish mystic Ramon Lull[31] who saw chivalry as akin to priesthood, with the 'Emperor' (i.e. the King – though indeed in some texts Arthur does become Emperor of Rome) taking a role similar to that of the Pope as titular head of *all* knights.

The Round Table itself came to represent far more than a meeting place for the Fellowship. Robert de Borron,[43] tracking backward again as he had done in the story of Merlin, added a further dimension. The Table of Arthur, he declared, was made in the likeness of two earlier tables. The first, at which Christ and the Apostles sat to celebrate the Last Supper, had been copied by the Grail Kings as a suitable resting place for the Holy Cup itself, of which they were guardians and keepers. Finally Merlin built the third table, at which the Fellowship would meet until the Grail itself appeared and sent them forth on the greatest quest of all, for which they had long been prepared.

Behind this idea lies another, subtler set of symbolic references. In the starry realms, according to many ancient traditions, met a council of mighty beings whose concern was with the execution of the divine plan of creation. They too sat at a round table, and when Merlin brought the stones of the Giant's Dance from Ireland, to create what we now know as Stonehenge, he made that circle in the likeness of the Starry Table.

It does not matter that we know Merlin did not build Stonehenge, for we are speaking the symbolic language of myth, built layer upon layer in the consciousness of humanity. Thus, Merlin built his circular temple on the Table of the Earth, a third dimension which completes the parallels with the imagery of Robert de Borron, and may be expressed thus:

TRADITIONAL	DE BORRON
Round Table of the Stars	Table of the Last Supper
Round Table of Arthur	Table of the Grail
Round Table of the Land	Table of Arthur

Fig. 2: The Three Tables

Thus not only is there a hierarchical relationship established, on the one hand, between the starry realms, the earthly kingship of Arthur, and the sacredness of the land; but so also is there a direct relationship between the mystical opening up of the Christian message, the expression of this in the Grail mysteries (see Chapter 6) and the Fellowship of the Round Table who were destined to go in search of the sacred vessel.

Thus within the Arthurian tradition are inner realities expressed by outer symbolisms. With the passing of the Fellowship on the terrible field of Camlan, nothing could be found to replace them. The country returned to the state of anarchy which had existed before the coming of Arthur; the Lands Adventurous faded from the minds of those who had once sought them out, and the Otherworld Forest was cut down. Yet the dream remained, as it does to this day. There are still those who would sit at the Round Table, to listen to the tales of the homecoming knights, and perhaps even brave an adventure themselves in the Otherworld realms of wonder.

EXERCISE 3: THE TABLE ROUND

The Table was ever a meeting place for those of like mind who desired to share the insights deriving from their adventures. So too should it become for all who pursue the path of the Arthurian tradition. Thus this next exercise is designed to enable the construction of an inner place where you may invite friends both inner and outer to share your own experiences and intuitions.

Begin by establishing the framework of the Lands Adventurous. See yourself standing, once again, in a high place, looking out across a country of great variety and richness such as you would wish to walk in and explore. Here adventures await you, meetings will take place that may change your whole life. For this is the inner realm of Logres, the ancient magical kingdom of Arthur, where all things are possible, and where the walls that separate the outer world from the inner are thin and transparent as glass.

As you look out across this wondrous land, you see the sunlight flash upon the roof of a building. Transport yourself now, in your imaginal body, to the entrance of that building, which seems to your inner vision to be a great circular hall, the walls of which are of crystal, so that it blazes with light like a great jewel.

At the door stands a figure in armour as bright as the sun. It is Sir Kay, the Seneschal of Arthur's court, of whom you must ask permission to enter. Do not be concerned at his crusty manner, for he was and is a great knight of the Round Table, and the beloved foster-brother of the king himself. If your reason for desiring entry is satisfactory – and you alone know whether it is so or not – you will be permitted to enter.

You find yourself inside the crystal walls, and there before you at the centre stands the Round Table itself, built of massive timbers, on which are carved many curious symbols and designs. Around the edge are ranked several rows of high-backed seats, on each of which is the name of the knight who sits there. On one of these is your name written, and Sir Kay will show you to your place at the Table.

At this point in your journey you must ask yourself an important question: what is your role in the mysteries of the Table? The answer you give will govern what you next experience, so be as honest as you can. It is not yet for you to sit down in the inner circle of places, with the great knights. That honour must be earned as it always was, and you will be given many opportunities to experience adventures and trials which will fit you in time for such a place.

For now you should watch, and listen, and learn. For as you take your place, you see that many of the seats are already filled by those who have gone before you. Many will have adventures to relate, insights to share, tales to tell. You may remain for as long as you wish, for here time is without meaning. Perhaps if you are lucky, the king himself will enter, or Guinevere come to listen to the latest adventures of her knights. And in time, you too will stand in your place, and feel the eyes of the assembled company upon you. Until that time, listen, learn, and above all remember.

When you are ready to depart, get up from your seat quietly and go from the crystal hall as you came, taking leave of Sir Kay as you do. He will remember you and welcome you again when next you visit the hall. Now let the image of the place and the landscape fade from your inner sight, and awaken and re-establish contact with the surroundings from which you began your journey. You may visit the hall of the Round Table as often as you wish, and each time you will learn more of it. In time you may wish to venture forth on adventures of your own, in which your inner guide will help and advise you (see Exercise 4).

4 · Goddesses and Guides:

Morgan le Fay and the Otherworldly Women

Then fearlessly and unhesitatingly Geraint dashed forward into the mist. And on leaving the mist he came into a large orchard; and in the orchard he saw an open space, wherein was a tent of red satin; and the door of the tent was open, and an apple-tree stood in front of the door of the tent; and on the branch of the apple-tree hung a huge hunting horn. ... And there was no-one in the tent save one maiden sitting in a golden chair, and another chaird was opposite to her, empty. And Geraint went ... and sat down therein.

Geraint, Son of Erbin from *The Mabinogion*

Goddesses Who Lead

There is a sense in which the majority of the women who appear in the Arthurian cycle are, or were, goddesses. That this is not immediately apparent is due to the gradual Christianisation of the material, and to changing attitudes of successive generations of storytellers, who altered, modified and sometimes suppressed many of the 'pagan' aspects of the tales they told.

Thus Morgan le Fay, whose origins have been traced to the Irish goddesses Macha and Morrighan, becomes, in the medieval Arthurian world, a mere enchantress – at least on the surface. Malory says of her that she was the daughter of Igrain and Gorlois of Cornwall, and that after her father's death, and the events of Arthur's birth engineered by Merlin, she was 'put to school in a nunnery, where she became a great clerk of necromancy'.[47]

It is easy to see in this statement a reference to earlier times, when female children who displayed a talent for the second sight, or other aptitudes for the mystical life, were sent to be educated by schools of priestesses such as once flourished in both Britain and Ireland. Morgan, who became known by the epithet 'le Fay', the Fairy, retained some of her goddessly qualities, even in the medieval tales.

Thus in Malory, while on the one hand she is portrayed as an enchantress and shape-shifter, Morgan also figures as one of the three mysterious queens who appear after the battle of Camlan to bear the wounded Arthur to Avalon, 'there to be healed of his wounds' and to await the time of his country's need.

Geoffrey of Monmouth, once again recording an ancient tradition, refers in his *Vita Merlini* to nine sisters who dwell on an island in the sea called 'the Fortunate Isle', or 'the Island of Apples'. He continues:

A Celtic Goddess by George Bain

> She who is first of them is more skilled in the healing art, and excels her sisters in the beauty of her person. Morgan is her name, and she has learned what useful properties all the herbs contain, so that she can cure sick bodies. She also knows an art by which to change her shape, and to cleave the air on new wings like Daedalus.[21]

Elsewhere in Malory, Morgan makes use of her shape-shifting ability, by turning herself and her followers into rocks when they are pursued by Arthur and his knights.

Geoffrey's description of the wondrous island, with its sisterhood of nine, conforms in every detail to other accounts of the Celtic Otherworld. It is clear enough that Morgan is the tutelary spirit, or goddess of this place, and that her animosity towards Arthur (who, as her half-brother, has faery blood himself) is merely an aspect of the challenging and testing role which such figures eternally offer, in order to discover who among their many servants is truly worthy of favour.

Morgan appears again in this guise in the marvellous Middle English poem *Sir Gawain and the Green Knight*,[18] where she is the organising principle behind the appearance of the monstrous green giant at Camelot. The story is typical of the role fulfilled by such goddessess in Arthurian literature, and is worth retelling for the light it throws upon them.

> The Court is assembled for the Christmas feast, but before it can begin there is a crash of thunder and in through the door rides a monstrous figure wielding a mighty axe. He is green from head to foot: green skin, green clothes, green horse. Mocking the assembly he offers to play 'a Christmas game' with anyone who has the courage. The rules are as follows: that he will receive a blow with his own axe from any man there, on the understanding that he will give one back afterward. At first no one comes forward, but when Arthur himself rises from his place, his young nephew Gawain steps forward to accept the challenge. He strikes a single blow, severing the Green Knight's head from his body. But to everyone's horror the giant picks up his head, holds it on high, and the lips move. He will expect Gawain in a year's time at the Green Chapel. Setting the head once more on his shoulders he departs as he came.
>
> A year passes and Gawain prepares to set forth to keep his word. He has no idea of the whereabouts of the Green Chapel, and his wanderings take him into the Wilderness of Wirrall, where he faces danger from trolls and the harsh Winter weather. Half dead from cold and fatigue he arrives at last at the castle of Sir Bercilak, a huge, larger than life figure who offers him hospitality and introduces him to his beautiful wife, who is accompanied by a hideous old woman. Bercilak declares that he knows where the Green Chapel is, a mere few hours'

ride away, and declares his intention of going hunting. When Gawain declines to accompany his host, preferring to rest, Bercilak proposes a sporting exchange of winnings: he will give Gawain whatever spoil he derives from the day's hunting, in exchange for anything his guest has won during the same period.

Once Bercilak has departed his wife enters Gawain's room and does her best to seduce him. Gawain politely refuses, but is forced to accept a single kiss. When Bercilak returns with the spoils of the hunt, all that Gawain has to exchange is the kiss. The same thing happens on the two successive days, with each time the lady of the castle amorously approaching her guest, and Gawain accepting first two then three kisses, which he duly exchanges with his host. On the third day, he confesses his errand, and that he has little chance of surviving, at which Lady Bercilak offers him a green baldric which protects its wearer from all harm. This Gawain accepts, with some hesitation, and does not declare it in his days 'winnings'.

Next morning he sets out for the Green Chapel, and on arrival finds the Green Knight sharpening his axe. Gawain kneels in the snow and his adversary twice feints, until Gawain is angered and bids him strike once and for all. The third blow merely nicks Gawain's neck, at which he leaps up declaring honour satisfied and calling on the Green Knight to defend himself. Whereat the giant laughs and says that the 'game' is over, and that he is really Sir Bercilak, enchanted into his present shape by the arts of 'Morgane the goddess', who is really the old crone at the castle. Her intention had been to frighten Guinevere, and to test the strength of Arthur's knights. Gawain has come through with honour unstained, except for accepting the green baldric from Lady Bercilak, for which reason he received the nick from the Green Knight's axe. Gawain returns to Camelot and tells his story. All the knights decide to wear green sashes in honour of Gawain's successful adventure.

In this extraordinary tale, which derives ultimately from an ancient Irish source, Morgan's role is made to seem slight by the poet, who sought a Christian allegory in what was, essentially, a pagan midwinter tale. (Yet even he called Morgan 'the goddess', as did at least two other medieval writers.)

I have dealt elsewhere with all of this in some detail[59] and will say here only that it is Morgan's presence which motivates the story, which concerns nothing less than an initiation designed specifically to test Gawain, and through him the Round Table Fellowship, and to prepare the hero for an even greater glory, when he becomes the 'Knight of the Goddess', her champion and lover in the realms of men.

This initiatory sequence is continued and completed in another poem of the same period (thirteenth century), *The Wedding of Sir*

Gawain and Dame Ragnall[23] in which, as already mentioned, Gawain is required to marry a hideously ugly hag, in order to save Arthur from death at the hands of the fearsome Gromer Somer Jour.

When, on their wedding night, Gawain suddenly finds that his hideous bride has become a ravishingly beautiful woman, he is given a further choice: to have her fair by night and foul by day, or vice versa. His response is to allow her to choose, and the spell is thus broken because Gawain gave her 'sovereignty', the right to be herself and to express her own nature – a rare enough thing in the repressive Middle Ages.

Behind this curious tale we catch a glimpse of an age-old theme, where the Goddess of Sovereignty herself encounters the new, young king of the land and by testing him proves his worthiness to rule. In the version outlined above Gawain acts as Arthur's surrogate, and is, at the same time, established as the Champion of the Goddess, who through him offers her blessing upon the land.

Her choice of Gawain, Arthur's nephew, is not out of place, since to the Celts the relationship of sister's son was considered of equal or even greater worth than patrimony. We may see in this a natural concomitant of the act where Arthur begets a child upon his half-sister Morgause. In the romances she is Morgan's sister, but it is easy to detect the presence of a single figure behind both – the Goddess of the Land, testing the young king. For whatever reason, in this instance Mordred, the offspring of this union, becomes Arthur's nemesis – perhaps because, in his pride, Arthur refused to acknowledge the right, by Celtic law, of his sister's son to rule. (In the same way, he ordered the head of the god Bran the Blessed, buried under White Mount in London to offer protection against invasion, to be dug up, on the grounds that he alone should ward the land from its enemies.)

THE FLOWER BRIDE AND THE DARK GODDESS

In *Gawain and the Green Knight* it is specifically stated that the reason why Morgan sent the Green Knight to Arthur's court was to frighten Guinevere. On one level the reason for this was an old rivalry, dating from the time near the beginning of Arthur's reign when Guinevere had banished one of Morgan's lovers from court, thus beginning long-term hostilities. On another there is quite of different sort of rivalry between the two – that of two goddesses of very different aspect.

Morgan, as her origin in the savage figure of the Morrighan indicates, is a dark goddess, representing the powerful earthy qualities of winter and warfare. Guinevere, on the other hand, who was also once a goddess, is of the type called the Flower Bride, representing spring, the unfolding of life, the burgeoning of growth. As such; these two are in polarised opposition for all time, and it is even possible to see, in the story of Guinevere's love for Lancelot, who becomes her champion and brings about the eventual ruin of the Round Table, a pattern of the elemental struggle between the champions of summer and winter for the hand of the Spring Maiden.

A version of this is told in the *Mabinogion* tale of Pwyll, who changes places for a year with Arawn, the Lord of the Otherworld, and undertakes, as one of Arawn's ritual tasks, an annual fight with Hafgan (Summer Song) for the possession of Creiddylad, the Maiden of Spring. We may judge the importance of this theme from the fact that echoes were still to be found as late as the nineteenth century in Wales, where teams of people led by a Lord of Summer and a Lord of Winter, engaged in mock battle for the Maiden.

Thus, in the Arthurian tales, Lancelot, who is Guinevere's champion, becomes the bitterest foe of Gawain, who is, as Knight of the Goddess, therefore Morgan's champion also. To begin with the two men are friends, and this lasts through many adventures until Lancelot accidentally kills Gawain's brother (significantly while rescuing Guinevere). Before this come numerous challengers who either insult the queen, accuse her of falseness to Arthur, or abduct her.

This last event is significant for a number of reasons. It is one of the roles of the Flower Bride to be stolen away by one of her suitors, and then to be rescued by the other – thus forming an endless shifting of polarities with each succeeding seasonal change. In the case of Guinevere we have a clear indication of her having at one time fulfilled this role in a story contained in the *Life of Gildas* by Caradoc of Llancarfan.[7]

In this text, which deals with the deeds of a sixth-century saint who may actually have known the historical Arthur, we read how Melwas of the Summer Country carried off Guinevere, who had then to be rescued by Arthur – though not without the intervention of the saint. This story reappears in several versions within Arthurian literature, where the abductor had become Meliagraunce, a knight who desires Guinevere for his own. Then, the rescuer is Lancelot, rather than Arthur, a seeming continuation of the various surrogate figures who stand in for the king at certain points in his life.

The identity of Melwas or Meliagraunce is not hard to fathom. In the *Life of Gildas* he is called King of the Summer Country – a name for the Otherworld. In the later versions Meliagraunce is the son of King Bagdemagus of Goirre or Gor, both names for the Otherworld. In the story of Pwyll he is identified as Arawn, King of the Celtic Hades. Hence we have a scenario in which Guinevere is carried off into the Otherworld by its king or his representative, to be rescued by her champion. The Flower Bride is brought back in triumph to the court of her lord, who is King of the Land.

We need only add to this the fact that, at an earlier stage in the development of the Arthurian tradition, Gawain was the queen's champion. In the later texts he has changed allegiance from one aspect of the goddess to another, and has thus become the *opponent* of the Flower Bride's champion. This is, of course, a vastly simplified scenario; each aspect of the goddess has its own multifarious aspects – as indeed we may see from the sheer variety of roles fulfilled by the various Otherworldly women in the Arthurian world.

THE INITIATORS

So many of these appear at Arthur's court, usually beginning as suppliants but ending as initiators, that it is not hard to perceive a clear pattern. One story in particular is worth summarising. This is Malory's 'Tale of Sir Gareth' from *Le Morte D'arthur*.[47]

The hero is Gawain's youngest brother, the son of Morgause and Lot of Orkney, but he chooses to remain incognito on his arrival at Arthur's court, and begs, as the first of three boons from the king, to be fed for a year. Kay, who takes charge of him, puts him in the kitchens and generally mocks him, naming him 'Beaumains', Fair Hands, because of his unusually large white hands. Both Lancelot and Gawain befriend him in that first year, though even the latter does not recognise his brother.

At the end of the year a damsel named Lynette appears asking for a champion for her sister against Sir Ironside, the Red Knight of the Red Launds, who is besieging her castle. Gareth, alias Beaumains now makes his two further requests: that he be given this adventure and that Lancelot should follow him and make him a knight when he deems the youth has earned it. Arthur agrees and Gareth and Lynette set out together, the maiden riding ahead and scorning anything to do with the 'kitchen knave' that King Arthur has seen fit to send with her.

During the succeeding days Gareth proves himself a sterling fighter, finally bringing Lancelot, who has followed, to a halt – at which point the great French knight declares Gareth a worthy opponent and knights him forthwith. Despite this, Lynette continues to upbraid her young escort, giving him the benefit of a tongue-lashing at every opportunity.

Gareth, however, staunchly refuses to be drawn and performs ever more extraordinary deeds of prowess as he encounters a succession of knights in variously coloured armour – finally defeating the Red Knight of the Red Launds himself and winning for himself the undying love of Lynette's sister Lyonors.

The story does not end there however. Lyonors bids her champion go forth to win even more honour before he marries her; then, when he has gone, changes her mind and requests her brother to lure him back again by pretending to kidnap a dwarf who has served him faithfully. All is reconciled and Gareth would have consummated his love before the wedding had not Lynette prevented it by magical means. Lyonors holds a great tournament in which Gareth wears a magic ring enabling him to change the colour of his armour at will. He thus fights several Round Table Knights incognito, then slips away unnoticed. Gawain sets out to discover the identity of the young knight who carried all before him and the two brothers meet and fight before Lynette arrives and stops them by identifying them to each other. She then heals their wounds with her magic and they return to the court, where Gareth is recognised as the son of Morgause and Lot and marries Lyonors at a splendid feast.

This story is one of several which tell of 'The Fair Unknown', generally the son of a great hero who appears at court incognito, has various adventures, fights with his own brother or father, and is finally recognised and honoured by all. In each of these there is also a figure not unlike Lynette, who performs the function of leading the hero through a series of adventures designed to test his skill and prowess. Almost without exception she possesses magical abilities and is active in arranging his eventual recognition.

Lynette herself actually appears as Lunete in another major story from the cycle, *Ywain* by Chrétien de Troyes. Here she rescues the hero several times from death and gives him a ring which conveys the power of invisibility. A passage from Chrétien's poem makes her true identity clear:

> I would like to make a brief mention of the friendship that was struck up in private between the moon and the sun. Do you know of whom I want to tell you? The man who was chief of the knights and honoured above them all should indeed be called the sun. I refer to my lord Gawain . . . And by the moon I mean she who is so uniquely endowed with good sense and courtly ways . . . her name is Lunete.[8]

Once again we recognise the figure of the goddess or Otherworldly woman who, once we have identified her, will be seen to appear in a hundred different guises throughout the Arthurian tradition. Her function is to guide and initiate tests and trials which bring about the transformation of the Round Table Fellowship from a simple chivalric order to a band of initiate knights. She it is who stands behind so much of the action and adventure in the stories – whether as Morgan le Fay sending a magical cloak which consumes to ashes anyone who puts it on, or as Ragnall, setting Gawain the supreme test of courtesy and love.

Such figures are an essential part of the inner dimension of the tradition. They are the initiators who cause things to happen, leaving the neophyte changed forever after. They are the polarised energy which drives the vast epic of Arthur from its dramatic beginnings to its climactic end. Without them the stories would be nothing more than a parade of meaningless images; with them they become a stately procession of wonders which open ever more and deeper doors into the landscape of the Otherworld.

EXERCISE 4: FINDING A GUIDE

If you have ever wondered about the practicality of working with the inner dimension of the Arthurian tradition, you will probably have considered making contact with an inner guide who can show you around this marvellous realm. There are a number of ways of acquiring such a guide; the following is only one example.

Begin by selecting a character from the cycle with whom you feel a rapport (a brief list of characters will be found at the end of the book). You may find that you resonate best with Sir Gawain, or with Guinevere, or with Arthur himself (do not be afraid to aim for such key figures; in the inner realms all are accessible). Be guided by the area you wish to explore – Arthur or Guinevere, or Sir Kay the Seneschal, or Bedivere the Butler would be particularly suitable in the instance of the court, although of course any knight or lady may travel to and from any house or castle. Galahad, Perceval or Bors lead naturally into the lands of the Grail. Do not feel constrained by the idea of crossing sexual boundaries: a man may learn a lot about his own feminine side by taking on a female inner guide, and the converse is true for a woman. Also, do not imagine that knights are for men and ladies for women. The Celts had an established tradition of female warriors and the women of the Arthurian world played an important role in the stories. Remember also that, as we have seen in the foregoing chapter, many were Otherworldly women to begin with, who consequently have a deep understanding of the inner realms.

Having selected your character, read everything you can find to do with him or her. If the present book has little to say of your choice, reference to the books listed in the Bibliography will assist you to look further.

When you feel that you really 'know' your character, intellectually, begin to meditate upon him or her, taking the following form. Build in the imaginal dimension a room, a building, or an outdoor scene. Then, when you have established this firmly in your consciousness, introduce the character of your choice into the scene. Sit down and talk with him or her or, if appropriate, go for a ride. Begin to explore the landscape of your imagining; you will soon find that the inner character will begin to take you to other places which you had not planned to visit. This means that your inner guide is firmly established and you should be able to work with him or her for as long as you wish.

Always remember, the men and women of the Arthurian tradition are archetypes, each with a different degree of power. Some may be less easy to work with than others, but you can always change to another character at any time, by simply taking formal leave of whichever inner guide you are with at the time, and then building again from the beginning.

On some occasions you may find yourself 'passed on' to another personage. This is an entirely normal process and may result in some interesting or profound relationships. Always remember that these people are friends in exactly the same way as people in the outside world, and will respond in a similar manner according to the way you treat them.

Should you ever find yourself in the position of wishing to give up the guide you have selected, but find for some reason that he or she refuses to leave, you should abandon all meditation for at least a week, and then begin again by consciously building the image of a new guide.

The resulting knowledge gained from this exercise will enable you to interact more fully with each stratum of the Arthurian tradition, as and when you come to study it. There is, in the end, no substitute for painstaking reading, but your inner guide will open to you an ever-deepening appreciation of the subject.

5 · LANCELOT AND TRISTAN:

TRUE LOVE AND PERFECT CHIVALRY

Ah! he wanders forth again;
We cannot keep him; now, as then,
There's a secret in his breast
Which will never let him rest.
          (Tennyson, *Idylls of the Kings*)

LOVE'S DANCE

There is a great deal about love in the Arthurian cycles, ranging from the openly sensual (what a seventeenth-century Puritan referred to as 'bold bawdy') to the deeply mystical. Treatment of the character of Gawain, who began life as a heroic figure dedicated to the service of the feminine principle (the goddess), and ended it as a libertine, exemplifies the way in which shifting cultural forces changed the way successive generations of writers chose to depict love.

To the Celts it was a joyful sport in which all men and women engaged as a matter of course. Sex itself was frequently depicted as a way of reaching a mystical relationship with the elements – hence the idea of Sacred Kingship and the marriage with the land; while countless meetings with 'Maidens of the Wells' engendered heroes who were more than half of the Otherworld. Many of the premier heroes of the Arthurian cycles originated in this way, including Arthur himself, Gawain, and both the great heroes dealt with in this chapter.

Indeed, if one is looking for proof of the Celtic origins of the Arthurian tradition one need look no further than the often complex love-lives of these two heroes – despite the fact that by the time the full glory of the literary heritage occured, during the Middle Ages, love had begun to be seen in a very different way: sometimes as a cult with all the trappings of religion, sometimes as a sinful occupation best expunged from the human system, and sometimes as a romantic experience which foreshadows the ideas of the eighteenth and nineteenth centuries.

Lancelot's literary origins are more vague than those of Tristan. He almost certainly derives from a character named Llwch Lleminiawg, who appears by name in the *Mabinogion* and in the poem *The Spoils of Annwn* already referred to. He carries a fiery sword and may thus be seen as a type of solar hero like Gawain, with whom he shares several other attributes. But other than these few sparse references nothing more is known of him until he reappears in a twelfth-century Swiss poem called *Lanzalet*,[37] in which the story of his childhood is more or less as in the version below, but in which he has yet to acquire his best-known role as Guinevere's lover.

Lanzalet is almost certainly based on a lost Celtic original, which must have told more of the early history of the hero, but for the rest we have recourse to medieval texts for a fuller account.

For Tristan, on the other hand, we have a more detailed set of reference. He may, indeed, have been a genuine historical personage, Drust or Drustan, son of Talorc or Tallwch. Evidence suggests that he was of Pictish origin, which possibly makes him older than any of the Arthurian heroes, since the Picts were an indigenous population in Britain before the coming of the Iberian Celts. Fragmentary references to his story, which involves his liason with the wife of March ap Meirchawn (the King Mark of later stories), are found scattered throughout Celtic literature. In the *Triads*[6] he is referred to as one of the 'Three Mighty Swineherds of the Island of Britain, who guarded the swine of March ap Meirchawn, while the swineherd went to ask Esyllt to come to a meeting with him'.

Apart from the fact that here we have a clear reference to the traditional triangular relationship between Tristan, Isolt and Mark, the association of Tristan with pigs, sacred to the Celtic Mother Goddess, is also noteworthy. since in each case, where the outward story of love and betrayal exists, there is a shadowy underpinning of Otherworldly characters, who reflect and influence the lives of the mortals in the outside world. If we look more closely at the histories of the two heroes we will see how this reveals itself at almost every point in their lives.

THE ILL-MADE KNIGHT

On the face of it there is little essential difference between the stories of Lancelot and Tristan. Both are born and raised away from their original homes and families; both are mighty fighters unequalled in their time; both are considered examplars of courtly love, the strange movement of the twelfth-century troubadours which made a virtue of love outside the bonds of marriage, and raised the service of lover to beloved to an almost religious fervour.

Yet there are differences, which become apparent when one examines their lives in greater detail. It is a difference, ultimately, between kinds of love, which each, in his way, represents.

Lancelot is the son of King Ban of Benwick and his queen, Elaine. Shortly after their son's birth Ban, who is one of the staunchest supporters of the young Arthur in the early days of his reign, becomes involved in a war with the neighbouring king, Claudas, who eventually overruns his lands and forces the rightful king and queen to flee. As they are escaping, Ban looks back to see his home in flames and the sight causes him to fall in a swoon from which he never rises. His queen, hurrying to his aid, leaves their son, who is then named Galahad, unattended for a moment only. In that time the Lady of the Lake appears and steals the child away to her palace beneath the waters. Heartbroken, Queen Elaine builds a church on the site of the hill where King Ban fell. The infant Galahad, now renamed Lancelot of the Lake, grows to manhood in the company of women and the faery-like mermen of the lady's palace. He learns quickly and develops great strength and skill in arms. He meets his cousins, Bors and Lional, and a half-brother named Ector, and when Lancelot reaches the age of eighteen, the four young men set out for Arthur's court and the famous Fellowship of the Round Table.

In memory of King Ban's support during his youth Arthur heaps favours on the newcomer, dubbing Lancelot a knight on St John's Day. In some versions of the story one of Lancelot's first tasks is to fetch Arthur's bride, Guinevere the daughter of King Leodegraunce, to Camelot for their wedding, and on this occasion the couple first begin to fall in love. In others texts Guinevere is already established when Lancelot arrives, and he soon becomes one of the Queen's Knights, a kind of sub-order of the Round Table to which young and aspiring knights were attached before they had fully proved themselves. Lancelot then begins a whole series of adventures which establish him beyond question as the greatest knight of his time. Among other deeds he conquers the dark custom of a castle named Dolorous Gard, which then becomes his own home and is renamed Joyous Gard. In the haunted graveyard of the castle Lancelot raises the lid of a great tomb which no-one else can move and finds written within his true name and lineage and a prophecy regarding his own son, whose name will also be Galahad.

Returning to Camelot he becomes a Knight of the Round Table and aids Arthur in putting down the rebellion of Galehaut the Haut Prince, who surrenders to Arthur after observing Lancelot's chivalry and fortitude in battle. He afterwards becomes Lancelot's closest friend and in an episode later made famous by Dante[11] acts as a go-between for the tongue-tied knight and the Queen whom he worships.

There follows the episode of the False Guinevere (see Chapter 1) during which time the real Queen takes refuge with Lancelot in Galehaut's kingdom of Surluse (possibly the Scilly Isles). After the discovery and death of the False Guinevere, Lancelot restores the real queen to Arthur, but by this time the couple are irrevocably in love, and from that moment Lancelot's life becomes an endless struggle with his conscience which leads him to pursue quest after quest in order to be away form the court and the Queen. On one such adventure he rescues a lady from a bath of boiling water in which she has been imprisoned by enchantment for several years. This is Elaine of Corbenic, daughter of King Pelles the Grail Guardian, and by means of a trick by which Lancelot is persuaded that he is visiting Guinevere, he engenders upon Elaine the son who is to be named Galahad and who will grow up to be the destined Grail winner. P.L. Travers has suggested that Lancelot may have taken a vow of celibacy when he could not love Guinevere. Thus the knowledge that he had not only betrayed his love for Guinevere but also broken this vow drove Lancelot mad for a time until he was eventually discovered wandering naked and starving in the forest, and nursed back to health by Elaine, with whom he returned to Joyous Gard for a time.

Soon after this begins the quest for the Grail, which will be dealt with more fully in the next chapter. Lancelot's part in this is ambiguous. The coming of his son Galahad sets the whole adventure in motion, and the two, father and son, establish a deep relationship which is, however, to be short-lived since Galahad dies at the end of the quest. Lancelot himself has several visions of the Grail, and finally comes to the very door of the chapel where the holy vessel is kept. But he is prevented from entering by an angelic presence and falls into a trance which lasts for several weeks. It is made clear to him, before the quest is at an end, that his failure is due solely to his love for the queen, which exceeds that for God, and for a time he is determined to renounce it. But, once the Grail quest is over, he resumes his old habits, and the seal is set upon the downfall of the Arthurian dream.

After the quest, with many of the older knights dead or lost, a younger contingent comes to the fore, and Mordred, Arthur's illegitimate son, begins to plot the destruction of the Fellowship. Capturing the lovers in the queens's chamber, just when they had reached a decision to end their long association for the good of the kingdom, Mordred forces Arthur to condemn his queen to the stake. Lancelot rescues her, but in the process accidentally kills Gareth and Gaheris, Gawain's brothers, thus instigating a war which is wished for by neither party but which ends in the death of Gawain and news that Mordred, left in charge of the kingdom while Arthur pursued Lancelot to his homeland in France, has declared his father dead and himself king. Returning, Arthur fights a last battle against his son and receives the wound which sends him to Avalon. Lancelot, hearing of all this, comes too late to the aid of his old friend. He visits Guinevere, now in a nunnery at Amesbury, one last time, and having taken leave of her puts aside his knightly weapons and armour to adopt the life of a hermit. As such he lives out his last days, finally hearing of Guinevere's death and not long outliving her. He is taken to be buried at Joyous Gard, while Guinevere is laid to rest beside Arthur. Lancelot's half-brother, Sir Ector, almost the last of the original Fellowship to survive, delivers the following elegy, which could be said to speak for all the knights, over Lancelot's body:

> 'Ah Lancelot', he said, 'thou are head of all Christian knights, and now I dare say', said Sir Ector, 'thou Sir Lancelot, there thou liest, that thou were never matched of earthly knights.' And thou were the courteoust knight that ever bare shield. And thou were the truest friend to thy lover

that ever bestrad horse. And thou were the truest lover of a sinful man that ever loved woman. And thou were the kindest man that ever struck with sword. And thou were the goodliest person that ever came among press of knights. And thou was the meekest man and the gentlest that ever ate in hall among ladies. And thou were the sternest knight to thy mortal foe that ever put spear in the rest.'[47]

Thus ends the story of the greatest of all Arthurian knights, and, perhaps, the most tragic. Lancelot is caught between the pull of love and duty, and in the struggle to maintain both, perishes, bringing down the kingdom with him. His failure in the Grail quest is one of the most painful stories in the entire cycle; so great is Lancelot's heart that he comes as near as any to achieving this most central of adventures. Yet he is not strong enough, and his failure is greater because of its narrow margin with success. His love for Guinevere proves stronger than his love for God, but it is a pure love in its fashion. Over the many years of his single-minded devotion to the woman he loves Lancelot never so much as looks at another (with the exception of Elaine, who tricks him into her bed). He is her rescuer on more than one occasion, her servant and even her slave. When he hurries to win her back from Meleagraunce he rides almost without hesitation in a cart – a vehicle reserved in those days for criminals, the dead or the transportation of dung – only to be condemned by Guinevere on arrival for having hesitated even as much as a second. Yet in the face of this and other occasions when the queen doubts his faithfulness, he remains staunch in his love.

These very human characteristics make Lancelot one of the most unforgettable people in the entire cycle, from whom much can be learned by those who seek to understand the importance of the Arthurian tradition.

THE SAD ONE

Tristan's story, though outwardly similar to Lancelot's is at heart very different. The son of King Meliodas and Queen Elisabeth of Lyonesse, he acquires his name (derived from the French *triste* (sorrow)) from the circumstances of his birth. His father having been stolen away by an enchantress, his mother, though heavy with child, goes in search of her husband, and gives birth to her son in the depths of the forest, where she soon dies. Thereafter, Tristan is brought up by a vassal of king Meliodas named Governal, until his step-mother tries to poison him so that her own sons may inherit. After this he is sent abroad in the care of Governal, where he is schooled in the courtly arts of hunting and hawking, and becomes an especially skilled harpist.

After a few years Tristan returns to Britain and visits the court of his uncle, King Mark of Cornwall. There he learns of an annual tribute of youths and maidens paid to the King of Ireland. He agrees to act as the king's champion and fights the gigantic Irish warrior known as the Morold on an island in the sea. He is victorious and slays the Morold, but in so doing receives a poisoned wound which refuses all treatment and soon begins to smell so badly that, on the advice of a wise woman, Tristan is set adrift in a small boat, in which manner he reaches Ireland. There he is taken to the daughter of the Irish king, who is named Isolt, and who is much skilled in healing. Calling himself 'Tantrist' and passing himself off as an itinerant harpist, Tristan is almost killed when Isolt discovers the real identity of her patient. The Morold had been her uncle and she has to be restrained from turning upon his slayer; but as the weeks pass her hatred turns to liking and finally to love as she spends time in the company of the young warrior.

The couple exchange rings before Tristan leaves Ireland to return to Mark's court, but once there he seems to forget Isolt because we next hear of him in rivalry with Mark for the favours of the wife of Segwarides. Perhaps because of this Mark turns against his young nephew and when pressure from his barons forces the king to look for a wife, he sends Tristan across to Ireland to seal the uneasy peace between the two countries by requesting the hand of Isolt of Ireland. Tristan has no difficulty in arranging this, since he had struck up a lasting friendship with Isolt's father King Anguish. But on the voyage home the couple drink a love potion, which was prepared by Isolt's mother and intended to ensure the success of Isolt's wedding with Mark, and they become lovers in earnest.

Brangane, Isolt's faithful servant, sacrifices her own virginity by pretending to be her mistress on the wedding night, and thereafter Tristan and Isolt begin a long affair, meeting on any and every occasion, devising an intricate system for passing messages, and continuing to cuckold Mark for a number of years, until a jealous knight named Andret gives them away and they are forced to flee. Taking up a wandering, idyllic life in the depth of the forest of Morrois, they are eventually discovered by Mark, who on seeing them sleeping with a sword between them (an accident rather than an intentional act) believes that he may have wronged the couple and offers to take Isolt back on condition that Tristan goes into exile.

Tristan and Isolt

Wandering into Britain the hero becomes a Knight of the Round Table, and soon proves himself equal to the very best of the Fellowship, at one time fighting even Lancelot to a standstill – though the contest remains inconclusive. The two become friends, but Tristan is soon driven to wander again, and in Brittany he takes service with King Hoel, whose daughter also happens to be called Isolt. Tristan becomes friends with her brother who persuades him to marry this

55

second Isolt; but the marriage is never consummated and shortly afterwards Tristan returns to Cornwall and steals the first Isolt away. They find refuge for a time in Lancelot's castle of Joyous Gard, until Arthur intervenes to persuade Mark to forgive them both and to take Isolt back once again. Returning to Brittany Tristan is wounded in a battle in which he fights on the side of King Hoel, and sends word to Isolt of Ireland to come and heal him. To the sailors who take this message he gives instruction that if they are successful they are to display a white sail, but that if Isolt refuses to come they should show a black. Isolt comes indeed, but her namesake, who loves Tristan deeply and is jealous of his great passion, tells him the sail is black. Whereat Tristan turns his face to the wall and dies. Isolt of Ireland, arriving to find her lover dead, lies down beside him and herself expires. They are buried in adjoining graves from which spring forth red and white briars which twine together in token of a love that reaches beyond death. Isolt of Brittany throws herself from a cliff and dies; Mark lives on to ravage Arthur's lands when the latter has passed to Avalon.[3]

THE TWO FACES OF LOVE

Tristan, 'the sad one', and Lancelot, 'the ill-made knight', span the entire gamut of passionate relationships, yet their stories, though essentially alike, are different in kind. Lancelot is essentially a man of honour, whose very real pain at the betrayal of the king he loves and serves makes him the most human of the characters in the cycle. From the very beginning, once he has recognised the love which he shares with Guinevere, he looses no opportunity to be away from the court – becoming, with each successive adventure, both more honoured and more desirable to women. yet despite himself he is helpless, returning again and again to the Queen like a falcon to the lure.

Tristan, on the other hand, is a more amoral figure altogether. We see him wooing Isolt and then next moment chasing the wife of Sir Segwarides. Later, after long years as Isolt of Ireland's lover, he is persuaded to marry her namesake of Brittany. Nor is he averse to playing all kinds of tricks upon Mark, including dressing as a beggar and carrying Isolt across a stream so that she can swear a public oath that no one else had ever laid a finger upon her.

Then there is the matter of the love drink, intended for Isolt and Mark. Much has been written about this and the effect it has upon the 'morality' of the tale. Is is quite clearly part of the earliest version of the story, and though some texts indicate that its efficacy was only for a period of five years, it is an essential part of the scenario. The question is whether it is the cause of the love between Tristan and Isolt, or whether their passion would have come about in spite of it. There can be no real answer to this; we can only look at the story as we have it and judge for ourselves. Despite which, a later text, the *Tavola Ritonda* (Round Table)[69] reports that Pope Agapitas (*sic*) granted indulgences to all who prayed for the souls of Tristan and Isolt, since it was the work of the potion which caused them to fall into sin!

Another aspect of the story which casts a different light upon Tristan's role is the character of Mark. Unlike Arthur, he is very far from a noble king, being not above giving Isolt into the hands of a band of lepers as a punishment for her betrayal of the marriage vows. He several times plans to have Tristan killed, and in at least one version of the story is partially successful, when one of his followers wounds the hero to death.[47]

But what can we learn from all of this, aside from the obvious moral lesson? How does the love of Lancelot for Guinevere, of Tristan for Isolt, fit in with the idea of chivalry? Malory, in a great and justly famous passage, makes the following observation:

> Like as winter rasure doth alway arase and deface green summer, so fareth it by unstable love in man and woman. For in many persons there is no stability; for we may see all day, for a little blast of winter's rasure, anon we shall deface and lay apart true love for little or naught, that cost much thing . . . But the old love was not so; men and women could love together seven years . . . and then was love, truth and faithfulness: and lo, in like wise was used love in King Arthur's days.

> (Bk XVII, Ch.25.)

The faithfulness of lover to beloved seems more important here than that of husband to wife, and indeed so it was held by a majority of people in a time when marriages were as a matter of course arranged for political reasons rather than for love. The teachings of the troubadours, who wandered through most of Europe during the time when the Arthurian tradition was at its height, are to be felt in almost every part of the stories of Lancelot and Tristan. For them, love was impossible between married people, and they placed the figure of the beloved on a pedestal from which it was not to be dislodged until the reactionary backlash of the seventeenth-century Puritan ethic. So strong became the movement known as Courtly Love that the church was forced to declaim against it – and this too is to be felt within the Arthurian stories, where a new kind of love, as portrayed by the quest for the Holy Grail, began to change the shape of the great love stories.

A CERTAIN INBORN SUFFERING

In the twelfth century, when Courtly Love was as its height, a clerk in the service of Marie de Champagne, daughter of the great Queen Eleanor of Aquitaine, composed a book of rules which codified the conventions governing the lover's every act. He called it *The Art of Courtly Love*[1] and gave a very different definition to that of Malory nearly three hundred years later:

> Love is a certain inborn suffering derived from the sight of and excessive meditation on the beauty of the opposite sex, which causes each one to wish above all things the embraces of the other and by common desire to carry out all of love's precept in the other's embrace.[47]

This certainly describes the intensity of passion evinced by both the great heroes and their queenly loves, though it fails to plumb the mystery which fuelled both. A third quotation, from the greatest medieval retelling of the Tristan story, by Gottfried von Strassbourg,[22] gives yet another dimension to it all.

In the story, the lovers have escaped and found refuge in the forest of Morrois, where they live an idyllic life together. Embroidering on the original version, Gottfried describes them as inhabiting a fantastic cave which he describes in intricate detail:

> The story tells us that this grotto was round, high, and perpendicular, snow-white, smooth, and even, throughout its whole circumference. Above, its vault was finely keyed, and on the keystone there was a crown most beautifully adorned with goldsmiths' work and encrusted with precious stones. Below, the pavement was of smooth, rich, shining marble, as green as grass. At the centre was a bed most perfectly cut from a slab of crystal . . . dedicated to the Goddess of Love. In the upper part of the grotto some small windows had been hewn out to let in the light, and through these the sun shone in several places.

> (trans. by A.T. Hatto.)

Gottfried interprets this fantastic place in some detail. It is round, broad, high and perpendicular etc. in token of love's simplicity, power and the aspiration which 'mounts aloft to the clouds'. The crown stands for the virtues of love, the whiteness and smoothness of the walls for its integrity, while the bed is of crystal in token of the transparency and translucency of all true love. Even the windows stand for 'Kindness ... Humility ... and Breeding', through which the light of honour shines.

Here then, love is still honour, even though the world would see it as otherwise. It is also joy, and offers an example which transforms others who hear of it. As Gottfried says:

> If the two of whom this love-story tells had not endured sorrow for the sake of joy, love's pain for its ecstasy within one heart, their name and history would never have brought such rapture to so many noble spirits.
>
> (ibid.)

In the end, then, human passion becomes inspiration, and we may see, behind even this, a deeper message, which leads back to the simpler times in which the stories were born. According to this way of seeing things, the human lovers are surrogates who allow the gods themselves to experience love in its every aspect. Through this they are better able to know the ways of mortals, and to strengthen the interaction between the worlds, keeping open the channels between the human and the divine.

Significantly, both Lancelot and Tristan love queens. A passage from the *Perceval* of Chrétien de Troyes, quoted by Jean Markale,[49] in which Gawain refers to Guinevere follows, making the significance of this, and of much within the stories of Lancelot and Tristan, clear:

> Just as the wise master teaches young children, my lady the queen teaches and instructs every living being. From her flows all the good in the world, she is its source and origin. Nobody can take leave of her and go away disheartened, for she knows what each person wants and the way to please each according to his desires.[49]

This is to say clearly what all the troubadours and their ilk were saying in every song and poem they wrote, that it is the divine element within all women which serves to fuel and inspire men to heights beyond their normal reach. Thus chivalry itself is informed by love, just as love is informed by the service required by all who take the vows of chivalry seriously. Love itself thus becomes an initiation, which is why we find so many of the women who feature largely within the Arthurian cycles to be of Otherworldly stock. We have seen that many of the heroes who court or worship or even marry them share this heritage also. So that, in the end, the worlds are brought together at every level, physical, emotional, and spiritual.

The last, represented by the quest for the Grail, shows another face of love.

EXERCISE 5: THE CAVE OF THE HEART

The cave described in the Tristan legend which became the refuge of the lovers was much more than a simple hollow carved out of the rock – it was a symbolic place to enter which was to inhabit a certain state of mind. A similar place exists, which is described as 'The Cave of the Heart', because it encompasses a deeply interior state in which compassion, at once the easiest and most difficult aspect of love to understand, is generated. The following exercise, therefore, should only be attempted by those who have reached a point of balance which enables them to view the world and the events of the world with a certain degree of detachment. From this dispassionate position it is possible to generate deeply felt love for the world and all who inhabit its confines.

See before you, a door, and behind the door a room, quietly lit, windowless, silent, in which all anger, fear, jealousy, distrust and hatred are left behind. Sinking deeply into meditation, become aware that there is a second person in the room with you, a tall and stately woman who sits with bowed head over an open book which rests on a desk before her. With this realisation comes another: that she is aware of you as you are of her, and that she is speaking to you, in words only you can hear.

What she says is for you alone to know, but it will be of some matter which is relevant to your deepest needs or feelings, the qualities which motivate you and cause your most profound understandings. For you must know that this is Guinevere the queen, who is also the Wounded Lady, just as Arthur is the Wounded King. Their wounds are not of the body alone, but of the spirit, and they are caused by the actions of all of humanity, who wound themselves and the world they inhabit, either knowingly or unknowingly, but always deeply.

Only one thing brings change and healing in the heart of the Wounded Queen, and that is compassion, a selfless desire for good which is the deepest level of all human loving, whether it is a wish to do something which will please the beloved, or a profoundly emotional response to the darkness which covers the face of the world from time to time. Discover, then, within your self, a desire to set right, to heal, a specific wrong, or trouble, of which you are aware, be it personal, global, or even cosmic. Concentrate upon this desire and it will be conveyed to the Lady Guinevere, and recorded by her in the book which lies before her. Only remember that this must arise from a selfless desire to bring about a change, not within the personality of the doer, but in the shaping and rhythm of the breathing cosmos. When you have finished, allow the sensations of the room and the presence of the Lady to fade, until you are again aware of the surroundings in which you began the meditation.

Take all the time your require for this work; return to it if you need again and again until you feel that some action has been set in motion. This is not an easy exercise, and may require some time before it begins to offer a response. Over a longer period of time its effects will begin to be felt, and with it the Cave of the Heart will be irradiated in such a way that you will become aware of the glow suffusing your daily life. For, as it is said in the circles of the mighty, 'There is a blessing upon those who serve.'

6 · THE GRAIL QUEST:

SPIRITUALITY AND THE SEARCH
FOR ABSOLUTES

When they were all seated and the noise was hushed, there came a clap of thunder so loud and terrible that they thought the palace must fall. Suddenly the hall was lit by a sunbeam which shed a radiance through the palace seven times brighter than had been before ... When they had sat a long while thus, unable to speak and gazing at one another like dumb animals, the Holy Grail appeared, covered with a cloth of white samite; and yet no mortal hand was seen to bear it. It entered through the great door, and at once the palace was filled with fragrance as though all the spices of the earth had been spilled abroad.

(*Queste del Saint Graal*)

THE CAULDRON OR THE CUP?

As the great contemporary visionary Dion Fortune wrote, almost fifty years ago, 'There are times in the history of races when the things of the inner life come to the surface and find expression, and from these rendings of the veil the light of the sanctuary pours forth.'[15]

The Lady of the Grail by Chesca Potter

Thus it was with the legends of the Grail. Too long ago now to identify with any degree of certainty, an idea found crystallisation in the form of a sacred vessel which contained the potentiality of all wisdom and knowledge, and through them of understanding. In ancient Hellenic mystery teachings it was the *Crater*, the Cup in which the gods mixed the very stuff of creation. The Sufis saw it as the Cup of Jamshid, from which knowledge and divine inspiration were dispensed. Its image is found in India, in Japan, in the Russias, and among the Celtic peoples, where it is recognised as the life-bestowing Cauldron belonging to the Goddess Ceridwen or the God Bran.

Then, sometime near the beginning of the eleventh century, perhaps influenced by the inner, magical history of the time, someone wrote a story which clothed either a Celtic or an Oriental tale in the dress and manners of the time. We do not know the identity of this writer, though tradition gives him a name at least – Blihis or Bliheris – singular among the writers of the Arthurian tradition for appearing as a *character* in a later text.[14] Whether he spoke of a Cauldron or a Cup we cannot know, since all traces of that story have vanished. Nor is it perhaps necessary to know which it was – or for that matter which influenced the other. Much controversy has raged over the nature and appearance of the Grail, whether it is a pagan symbol or a Christian image. But in the end such speculations are fruitless, taking one away from the essential meaning of the story rather than further into it. There are indeed aspects of the Grail which seem to reflect the wonder-working Cauldron; and there is that about the Cauldron which seems to prefigure the medieval accounts of the Grail. Whatever the truth, it is in these later, generally Christian versions of the story, that its true power is revealed.

THE PERFECT FOOL

Nevertheless, the first written story of the Grail which is still extant makes it neither pagan nor Christian – though it is possible to interpret it in either way.

About 1280, Chrétien de Troyes, already famous for his poems on various aspects of the Arthurian tradition, began work on his final romance, *Perceval, of the Story of the Grail*[8] He died before finishing it, and left an enigma which has exercised the minds and haunted the dreams of countless seekers after wisdom

ever since. The story he told may be summarised briefly as follows:

Perceval is brought up in the forest by his mother, who having lost a
husband and three other sons in battle is determined that her remaining
child shall know nothing of war or contest of arms. Then one day
Perceval encounters three of Arthur's knights and, mistaking them
at first for angels because of their shining armour, learns something
of the world of men. From this moment nothing will do but that
he must leave home in search of adventure. Despairing, his mother
clothes him in poor clothes, mounts him on a spavined horse and arms
him with a cooking-pot helmet and roughly fashioned spears, in the
hope that his foolish appearance will prevent him from encountering
any serious harm. She also tells him that if he should encounter any
women on the way he should take a ring and a kiss from them, but
nothing more.

Perceval's first encounter is with the Damsel of the Tent, who reacts
somewhat adversely when he follows his mother's advice. Forced to
flee from her jealous lover, Perceval nevertheless does not forget her.
Arriving at Arthur's court he is in time to witness an insult to the queen,
when a knight spills wine over her and steals her cup. Determining to
take this as his first adventure Perceval sets out in pursuit, easily kills
the knight and is in the process of trying to boil the remains in order
to obtain his adversary's armour, when he is discovered by an older
knight named Governal. This man virtually becomes a father-figure to
the young Perceval, and over the next months trains him in the manners
and mores of chivalry. Before they part he gives Perceval a second piece
of advice: never to speak out of turn or ask foolish questions for the sake
of curiosity.

It is this which effects Perceval's next adventure, when he stumbles
upon the Castle of the Grail, whither he is directed by a man fishing
from a small boat, who turns out to be his uncle. Within the castle
Perceval witnesses a mysterious procession, in which a candelabrum,
a spear which drips blood from the point, and a mysterious object called
a 'graal', are borne through the hall. In an inner room an ancient man
lies, seeming close to death, but who is kept alive by food provided by
the 'graal'.

None of this is explained and Perceval, mindful of Governal's advice,
forbears to ask its meaning. He goes to bed and next morning wakens
to find the castle vanished and himself sleeping on stones. He is then
challenged by a hideously ugly maiden, who accuses him of failing to
take advantage of an opportunity for great good. Outcast and wretched,
Perceval wanders for a long while in the wilderness, until he happens to
meet a group of pilgrims who remind him that it is Good Friday, when
all good Christians should make confession and attend the celebration
of the Eucharist.

Making his way to a hermitage in the forest, Perceval learns of the death of his mother, who died of grief when he failed to return or send word of his adventures. Filled with remorse Perceval prepares to set out again in search of the mysterious castle of the fisherman. The story then turns to the adventures of Gawain, who is also in search of the Grail; but half way through this part of the story the narrative breaks off in mid sentence, leaving everything unexplained.

So great was the power of this mystery that no less than four other writers attempted, with varying degrees of success, to complete Chrétien's story. Long before they did so, however, other, possibly independent versions appeared. We have already seen how Robert de Borron wrote a trilogy of works in which he attempted to fill in the missing parts of the story. In doing so he made the identification of the Graal or Grail with the Cup of the Last Supper, and thus made the story for all time part of Christian tradition. That he may not have been the first to do so is not important (he makes the statement that he is following another text); it is his version of the story that is remembered, and which probably sparked off a succession of further narratives in which the story of the Grail reached a level of detail and power probably undreamed of by either Chrétien or Robert – and most certainly by the mysterious Blihis.

Perceval, the 'Perfect Fool', was established as the champion of the Grail, and several stories of increasing complexity extended his role and attempted to explain the meaning of the Grail in bewildering detail. New dimensions were added at every point. The Grail Guardian became one of a family of such people, descended from Joseph of Arimathaea, the rich Jew who gave up his own tomb to house the body of Christ and was said to have received the Grail – and its secret teachings – from the risen Messiah in person.

Somewhere along the way someone explained the reason for the ancient king's infirmity by declaring him the victim of a blow struck, either accidentally or as the retribution for some great wickedness, by the knight Balin the Savage – seen by some as a representative of paganism. This became known as the Dolorous Blow, and not only did it cause an unhealing wound which could only be set right by the destined Grail winner, but also laid waste the Kingdom of the Grail Family, which became a desert place in which the most terrible adventures and tests of the quest took place. This too would only be made whole when the Grail Knight came and asked a ritual question which would set in motion a chain of events: the healing of the King, the fructification of the dead land, and something else, less tangible than either of these actions, which would somehow bring transformation to the whole world.

It is this 'something' that has occupied the energies of countless seekers ever since. For within the Grail is seen to reside healing for *all* the ills of creation. With its finding, or with the experience that comes to those who discover its innermost secrets, comes a release of energy, of selfless love and service, which could change the world for all time – perhaps even bring about the end of time, the rolling-up of the great cosmic chart upon which the history of humanity is written.

THE HOLY BLOOD

The single most important element to be added to the story of the Grail was its association with the Christian Eucharist. This shaped and influenced virtually every version which followed. The Grail was, quite simply, seen as an outward symbol of Christ's ministry, of the great sacrifice which brought God and man into closer proximity than ever before. Look at it however one will, it is the unique element of the Eucharist, the *direct* communion with the Godhead, which makes the Grail different from any similar hallowed or sacred object. From the point of the Incarnation, one may look forward or backward in time without losing sight of the essential fact: the Grail which became the object sought by the Knights of the Round Table, and subsequently by men and women from all walks of life and in all ages, once contained Holy Blood of the New Covenant, caught by Joseph of Arimathaea as he helped wash the body of Christ after the deposition from the Cross.

There is no getting away from this, however one chooses to inter-pret or reinterpret the Grail. It can be, and often is, all things to all men. It is a mutable image, which can be turned this way and that while remaining unchanged.

This does not mean that one has to be a believer in the Christian dispensation, any more than it requires that one should become a pagan. The Grail simply *is*, whatever we believe or do not believe. And it is this which makes it an utterly universal symbol, capable of the widest possible application. It has about it the stuff of mystery; it is also concerned with sacrifice, service and the search for the absolute, whether one calls this God or Goddess, Divine Spark, or by some even more abstract term.

The fact remains, no doubt, that there are similarities between the Celtic, pagan implements and the Christian chalice. These are clearly not accidental. One may assume, however, that poets and writers of romances like Chrétien de Troyes and Robert de Borron, as well as all the others who came after them, knew what they were doing. Possibly they were uncertain as to the origins of much of what they wrote. It is equally possible that they knew exactly whence it came. They were, however, first and foremost, creators, not men acting under supernatural guidance or (in many cases) especial piety.

That they were, at the same time, devout, is probable; most men were in the Middle Ages. They must have been aware that the Grail was uncanonical, even though it pertained to the heart of the Christian mystery.

The truth is that the image of the Grail continued to change, subtly, throughout the marvellous hundred years between the beginning and end of the eleventh century in which the greatest texts were composed. Chrétien's Grail is enigmatic, unfocused; his continuators, seeing fresh applications, added something to it. Robert de Borron took it back through time and space to Palestine, adding the dimensions of Joseph of Arimathaea, the Holy Blood, and the bringing of the Cup to Britain. The *Vulgate Cycle*,[71] compiled by Cistercian monks, possibly at the behest of the great theologian Bernard of Clairvaux, further deepened the theology by the introduction of various wandering hermits, who interpreted the dreams and visions of the Grail knights, deepening the realisations contained within them. Others, known and unknown, extended the pattern to include all that we now recognise as part of Grail mythology.

The reason why the twelfth century should have been such a formative period in the history of the Grail may in part derive from the fact that this was still an age of comparative doctrinal freedom. Though by no means free to believe whatever they chose, men were less threatened than in succeeding ages. In 1200 there were still some thirty years to go before the Inquisition was established, and a further fifty after that before the use of torture against suspected heretics was sanctioned by the church.

Once the belief in so-called 'new' ideas was considered heretical, something of the original and striking imagery was lost from the Grail romances written thereafter. Had it not been for the work of an unknown Cistercian, who wrote most if not all the section of the *Vulgate Cycle* dealing with the Grail, the myth might well have withered and died. As it was, with the creation of a new character (or at least, his development far beyond any original scope) the whole direction of the Grail legends was changed. Galahad, the Perfect Knight, child of Lancelot and the Grail Princess, had but one destiny: to find the Castle of the Grail and bring about the healing of the Waste Land.

THE PURE KNIGHT

The entry of Galahad into the Arthurian tradition is something of a minor miracle; one which Charles Williams, the greatest modern interpreter of the Grail myths, described as one of the most significant literary events of all time. The unknown author of the third part of the *Vulgate Cycle*,[67] realising the need for a new element to bind the stories into a coherent whole, hit upon the idea of bringing in a Christ-like figure who would literally 'redeem' the legends of their pagan origins. Thus Galahad was born: the sinless, stainless knight best known from Tennyson's nineteenth-century poem as declaring 'my strength is as the strength of ten, because my heart is pure'.

This statement does indeed seem to sum up the character of Galahad, whose name is full of Biblical resonance. It means, literally, 'a heap of testimony' and is understood as referring to the 'accumulated testimony of the Prophets to Christ as Messiah',[43] or, as we might perhaps put it, the focal point in the heritage of the tradition. Certainly his coming to the court of Arthur is redolent with New Testament detail:

> In the Meanwhile came in a good old man, and an ancient, clothed all in white, and there was no knight knew from whence he came. And with him he brought a young knight, both on foot, in red arms, without sword or shield, save a scabbard hanging by his side. And these words he said: 'Peace be with you, fair lords.'
>
> (Malory, Bk XIII, Ch. 3.)

All the seats of the Round Table are filled on this occasion, the 454th anniversary of the first Pentecost, with the exception of the Siege Perilous, which had remained empty and veiled since the founding of the Fellowship. Now it is uncovered, and the name Galahad is found to be written upon it in letters of gold. The young knight in red armour takes his place and the mysteries of the Grail begin in earnest; the greatest quest and adventure which the Round Table Knights were ever to attempt. Many would fail, including the great Lancelot. But Galahad is his son, born through an extraordinary substitution, whereby the greatest knight of Arthur's realm engenders the perfect knight on the Princess of the Grail, believing her to be Guinevere.

This in itself is a mystery of great profundity. Guinevere is an aspect of the Great Goddess, the Flower Maiden who rules over the springtime rebirth of the land. She is also the Sorrowful Queen, the Wounded Lady who suffers the burden of evil acts carried out in ignorance of love within the kingdom of Arthur. He, in turn, is the Wounded Lord. the very personification of the land over which he rules – Logres, the mystical realm *within* the geographical boundaries of Britain.

One may see, here, links in a causal chain which ultimately bring about the failure of Arthur's dream. Rightly, Galahad should have been the son of Arthur and Guinevere, king and queen, lord and lady. But Arthur begets Mordred upon his half-sister Morgause, and Lancelot is the queen's lover. Thus out of the tangled web of deceit and falsehood comes the redeeming figure of Galahad allowed, by a dispensation of light, to achieve the mystery of the Grail – though not, alas, to bring about the final transformation which would have established Logres as an earthly paradise. Instead, it is given to him to look within the Grail, at which point he expires in an ecstasy of desire which can no longer keep him from union with the absolute. It is left to Perceval, the Perfect Fool, to make possible the continuance of the Grail quest for later ages, and to Bors, the ordinary man and the third of the successful quest knights, to return with word of the great events to which he was witness.

Malory's account, based on the great *Vulgate Quest of the Holy Grail*,[43] is a magnificent parade of images. The knights, departing from Camelot in the ardour of the quest; their many and extraordinary adventures; the three successful knights who sail on the magical Ship of Solomon, voyaging through time to carry the Grail to Sarras, the Holy City in the east; the failure of Lancelot, of Gawain, and of many others; the sorrowful fate of Perceval's virgin sister, who gives her life-blood for a sick woman, and whose body is carried to the Holy City where she will be interred with Galahad; the return of Perceval to the empty Castle of the Grail, to allow the mystery to begin again – all this and more moves like a dream through the consciousness of those who begin the quest.

For those who go in search of the Grail today do so, whether they know it or not, in the wake of the Arthurian knights, who paved the way and sought the meaning within the great mystery in an open-hearted fashion. They set forth, knowing nothing of the perils that awaited them; and even as word of successive failures reached their ears, they continued the search unabated, establishing new paths, setting out fresh way-markers for those who would follow.

In this, they were far more than characters in a literary cycle of tales. They embodied a series of primary archetypes which have perhaps never been assembled in such a way again; they represent the whole spectrum of human experience, aspiration, failure and ultimate achievement.

Anyone who thus attempts the Grail quest today would do well to study their words and deeds, their successes and failures, as fully as possible. For therein lies much of the teaching of the wise, filtered through a thousand different paths and prejudices, into a great pool of knowledge which lies waiting for those with the courage to plunge into it. Those who do so will perceive many wondrous things – not least of which is a dawning understanding of the mystery behind the Arthurian tradition as a whole, which can only be partially glimpsed until this point is reached.

Once again it is the sheer *applicability* of the image that gives the Grail such universal relevance. It is not required that those who follow the Grail today adhere to any specific creed or cult – only that they seek the general good, the healing of the barren lands. These things are recognisable and desirable objectives, by whatever terms. Their very enactment causes changes within those who participate in them. By serving, we are served. We grow. The Grail encompasses us with its light and an exchange takes place between it and us. In allowing ourselves to be part of its action of healing or redemption, we ourselves partake of its blessing.

This is the great secret of the Grail – which is no secret at all – another paradox in its endlessly paradoxical nature. Everywhere and nowhere, it is sought by many, found by only a few. It has been several times withdrawn, yet it still remains. It can heal and it can destroy. It is God and yet not-God. It is a container which is worth far less than what it contains. Of its history, there seems no discernible beginning, no assured middle, no foreseeable end.

The Grail thus represents the most profound puzzle in the whole of the Arthurian tradition. It is dealt with elsewhere in more detail[58] – here is has only been possible to touch upon some of its mysteries, which are there to be discovered by contemporary seekers, who follow it down the deep ways of the heart, into the realms of wondoer and aspiration. There they are met by those who have trodden the way before, whose loving service has led them to stand as foster-parents to those who come after in search of the wisdom of the Grail. This, of itself, has no ending. It is eternal, as the quest itself is eternal. It offers wholeness in the midst of fragmentation. It binds together all who are of its family and its fellowship. It is a gateway between worlds, and a bridge to the Divine.

EXERCISE 6: THE CHAPEL OF THE GRAIL

No.quest is ever easy or lightly adopted. No matter what its objectives, or whatever high ideals fuel the journey, there are bound to be moments of doubt, of uncertainty, or of opposition. The following exercise is intended to enable the seeker to deal with such moments as efficiently as possible – though is must be remembered that the final success or failure of the endeavour lies as much with the interior state of the seeker as with any outside agency. There are many ways into the lands of the Grail, and this too, though difficult, can be one such way.

Closing your eyes and allowing yourself to sink deeply into meditation you awaken in a forest of great old trees. The sunlight of a summer's day strikes through the leaves and makes patterns on the earth. You walk along a wide, well-trodden path which leads to a clearing. In the centre is a small stone-built chapel, which seems deserted. The air is still; only the drone of bees and an occasional subdued bird-call breaks the silence.

You stand for a while before the entrance to the chapel until you feel ready to enter, then push open the rough wooden door and go within . . . It is cool and dim inside, with a feeling of long neglect – yet the floor is swept and the altar decked with flowers. You may feel constrained to kneel, or simply to stand with bowed head before the altar, and at this time certain realisations about your reasons for being in quest of the Grail may become known. Whatever these may be, good or bad, they must now be faced directly if you are to continue . . .

Time passes. You are not sure how long you have stood there in the empty chapel before you feel sudden warmth upon you and find that the sun has crept round until a ray of its lights falls through the narrow window behind the altar and alights on the spot where you are standing. Yet this light seems more than just the daily light of the sun – it passes deeply into you, warming not just body but the very spirit within. You feel saturated in light.

Slowly, as you bask in the glory of the light, you become aware of something upon the altar which was not present before. A simple cup is set there, but from it flows such energy and beauty that you know it is the Grail. Then, as you stand in awe, a cloud obscures the sun and the chapel is suddenly cold and dark. In the half-light you see a strange and terrible thing: a great dark arm and hand are pushed through the wall and reach towards the cup. You are powerless to move, however much you wish to; but you may summon the light by an affirmation of love and will to heal all hurt and wounded things. Make that affirmation now . . .

The cloud moves away from the face of the sun and the light is restored. As it strikes again into the heart of the chapel, the cup ignites in answering glory, and the grasping hand dissolves in dark smoke. Once again the chapel of the Grail is a still and peaceful place, and you see now something which was hidden from you before – a small door behind the altar. It stands slightly ajar, and through it you catch a glimpse of a garden filled with flowers. Somewhere you hear a distant note of music, which seems to call you . . .

You may follow that call, if you so desire. It will lead you into the country of the Grail, where you may walk and dwell for a timeless time until you are ready to return. You have but to imagine yourself back again in the forest, with the great trees rising on all sides and the sunlight penetrating their leaves in dazzling patterns . . . Awaken, then, from your journey, and know that if you have found your way into the place of the Grail this way will ever be open to you if you so desire it, and that if you did not choose to follow the way on this occasion you may do so again by visiting the chapel and passing through the narrow door which is no longer hidden.

7 · AVALON AND THE FAERY REALMS:

PATHS TO THE LAND BEYOND

And I will fare to Avalun, to the fairest of all maidens, to Argante the queen, an elf most fair, and she shall make my wounds all sound; make me all whole with healing draughts. And afterwards I will come again to my kingdom, and dwell with Britons with mickle joy.

Layamon, *Brut*

THE DREAM OF THE OTHERWORLD

It is virtually impossible to explore any of the traditions relating to Arthur and the Grail without encountering some aspect of the Otherworld. The knights in their wanderings continually stray out of the realms of men into the faery world, or else encounter the denizens of the Hollow Hills who have emerged with the intention of testing all whom they meet. Why they should seek to do this has never been successfully answered. In part it seems to be out of nothing more than a sense of pure mischief; but at a deeper level it appears that the people of the Otherworld, in their shy way, actively *seek* the companionship of men – though they are less willing to share the secrets of the inner realms or to give power to mortals.

Doorway to the Otherworld

In one of the many stories featuring Gawain, who has a relationship with the Otherworld perhaps unique among the knights, he meets a dangerous figure called the Carl of Carlisle. Gawain accompanies him on a journey which takes them at once inside the Hollow Hills, where they seem to travel though a world as real as the one they have left, save that the adventures which follow are touched with a degree of strangeness unusual even for the Champion of the Goddess.[59]

In another text, *Sone of Nausay*,[44] the hero, who is pictured as a genuine historical personage, possibly from the region of Alsace, journeys with the King of Norway through a land filled with strange creatures, to an island where they find the body of Joseph of Arimathaea, perfectly preserved, together with the Grail itself! The setting is wholly Otherworldly, however, and the island, which is named

Galoche (probably a corruption of the French word for 'Welsh') is one among many such Otherworldly places found throughout the Arthurian and Celtic traditions.

Merlin, also, had his island retreat, sometimes located at Bardsey, off the coast of Anglesey. Here he was believed to have his observatory, and to guard the Thirteen Treasures of Britain, which included an inexhaustible cauldron, a collection of magical weaponry, and a great horn which had once belonged to the god Bran – who also, incidentally, had an island where time stood still and where food and drink were provided from an unseen source.

Each of these places represented a deep-seated urge for Otherness, for a place where the laws of the natural world no longer obtained; where anything was possible, and even the poor might become rich, or the dispossessed get back their lost standing in the eyes of the world. Later, this dream was to be replaced by another – that of Heaven, the paradisial place where the good were assured of an eternity of rest and peace. The Celtic Otherworld was altogether a more robust place, where the simplest pleasures – ample food and drink, beautiful women, great combats in which neither opponent received fatal wounds – abounded. One place above all summed up this Otherworldliness more than any other: Avalon.

THE ISLAND OF APPLES

Among all the hundreds of names attached to the Celtic Otherworld, that of Avalon must be the most evocative. It is the place to which tradition ascribes the last resting place of Arthur. There he waits still for the day when he is called back to serve the needs of the land, to begin again the work that was left unfinished after the ending of the Grail quest and the bloody slaughter of the Round Table Fellowship at Camlan.

Many have sought to discover the whereabouts of this fabled place, and tradition has, since the Middle Ages, associated it with the Somerset town of Glastonbury, which has been called 'this holiest earth'. Here Joseph of Arimathaea is believed to have come, bearing the precious Grail, and to have established the first Christian community there within living memory of Christ. And here saints such as Patrick, Bridget and Columba are said to have lived for a time.

It may be unwise to seek a physical place for something as elemental as Avalon, but before Glastonbury (a Saxon name), in the time of the Celtic war-lords when Somerset was known as 'The Summer Country' and was more than half in the Otherworld, the site was known by another name, *Yniswitrin*, which has been interpreted as meaning 'The Island of Glass', ruled over by Avalach, who is also called *Rex Avalonis*, King of Avalon. He it is who is the father of Morgan, described in another text as 'The Royal Virgin of Avalon – though that title can be only that of a hereditary guardian rather than a literal description.

So *Yniswitrin* became Avalon, the Island of Apples, a place of wonder and mystery, where it was known that some great and mysterious object was kept, guarded, perhaps by a college of priestesses under the leadership of Morgan – she who was elsewhere known as Arthur's sister and a servant of the Goddess.

Thus an inner landscape was outlined within the Arthurian tradition. Logres, the mystical heart of Britain, with its royal castles at Camelot, Caerleon and Carlisle, its great forests in which the Fellowship of the Round Table wandered in search of adventure, its magical springs and wells guarded by Otherworldly maidens of surpassing beauty. And at the centre, somehow, lay Avalon, the magical isle which was a doorway onto the lands of faery, to the people of the *Sidhe*, who sent forth their representatives into the lands of men, to try and test them – and sometimes to lead them back into the deep places of the earth, where the Old Gods still dwelled, as they had done since the beginning of time.

The Arthurian kingdom was always on the edge of faery. When Arthur set out in his ship *Pridwen* with his band of wondrously endowed warriors, they sailed to an island where the Cauldron of Rebirth was kept, guarded by nine muses, and by the warriors of the Otherworld. Nor a far cry from this to another island, ruled by Morgan and her sisters, where a vessel was housed that could give life and healing to those in sore need.

But Avalon was more even than this. It was a place where eternity touched the earth, where anything could happen – and did. It was both a gateway between the worlds and the home of the deepest mysteries of Britain. It was one of 'The Fortunate Isles', a place of apple trees and the perfume of flowers. Malory calls it 'the vale of Avilion', and Geoffrey of Monmouth describes it in detail.

> The island of apples ... gets its name from the fact that it produces all things of itself; the fields there have no need of the ploughs of the farmers and all cultivation is lacking except what nature provides. Of its own accord it produces grain and grapes, and apple trees grow in its woods from the close-clipped grass. The ground of its own accord produces everything instead of merely grass, and people live there a hundred years or more. There nine sisters rule by a pleasing set of laws

77

those who come to them from our country . . . Thither after the battle of Camlan we took the wounded Arthur . . . Morgan received us with fitting honour, and in her chamber she placed the king on a golden bed and with her own hand she uncovered his honourable wound and . . . at length she said that health could be restored to him if he stayed with her for a long time and made use of her healing art.

(trans. J.J. Parry.)

This Avalon is a place of healing, a realm of peace where even the enmity of Morgan for Arthur no longer holds good. Here, too, belongs Nimue, the damsel of the lake who enchanted Merlin and finally imprisoned him in a cavern beneath a great rock. The Queens of Norgales and of the Waste Land are said to come here, connecting the Otherworld with the Kingdom of the Grail.

Another text, the *Gesta Regum Britanniae*,[64] which actually post-dates Geoffrey by a few decades, describes Avalon in terms which link it even more explicitly to the realms of faery.

This wondrous island is girdled by the ocean; it lacks no good things; no thief, reiver or enemy lurks in ambush there. No snow falls; neither Summer nor Winter rages uncontrollably, but unbroken peace and harmony and the gentle warmth of unbroken Spring. Not a flower is lacking, neither lilies, rose nor violet; the apple-tree bears flowers and fruit together on one bough. Youth and maiden live together in that place without blot or shame. Old age is unknown; there is neither sickness nor suffering – everything is full of joy. No one selfishly keeps anything to himself; here everything is shared.[52]

In other cultures this would have been called an earthly paradise; to the Celts it was the Otherworld, a place as simple and real as any one might find in the realms of men. We may wonder at a realm where sickness and sorrow, old age and misery are banished; where men and women live together in peace and harmony, and where all things are provided from the goodness and plenty of the earth. To the people who helped create the Arthurian tradition as we know it such places lay merely over the next hill, or behind the next tree.

I went in the twinkling of an eye
Into a marvellous country where I had been before.
I reached a cairn of twenty armies,
And there I found Labraid of the long hair.

I found him sitting on the cairn,
A great multitude of arms about him.
On his head his beautiful fair hair

Was decked with an apple of gold.
Although the time was long since my last visit
He recognised me by my five-fold purple mantle.
Said he, 'Wilt thou come with me
Into the house where dwells Failbe the Fair?'

At the door toward the West
On the side toward the setting sun,
There is a troop of grey horses with dappled manes,
And another troop of horses, purple-brown.
At the door toward the East
Are three trees of purple glass.
From their tops a flock of birds sing a sweet drawn-out song
For the children who live in the royal stronghold.
At the entrance to the enclosure is a tree
From whose branches comes beautiful and harmonious music.
It is a tree of silver, which the sun illumines;
It glistens like gold.

There is a cauldron of invigorating mead,
For the use of the inmates of the house.
It never grows less; it is a custom
That it should be full forever.
There is a woman in the noble palace.
There is no woman like her in Erin [Ireland].
When she goes forth you see her fair hair.
She is beautiful and endowed with many gifts.[10]

This seems a wholly fitting resting place for Arthur, who sought to create just such a perfect realm in the world, only to be defeated by human weaknesses and failings of a kind to which the people of the Otherworld were not subject.

THE WONDROUS REALM

Avalon, then, is like the perfect, balanced state of being, reached sometimes in meditation, or with the practice of certain religious disciplines. It is a place sought at once by those in quest of the Grail and of the Cave of the Heart; or as Dion Fortune put it: 'Sir Lancelot seeking one thing and Sir Galahad another, still they come to Avalon.'[15] It is the heart from which all the Arthurian mysteries are generated – and to which all who seek to know and understand those mysteries must come in the end.

Here, at the Round Table of the Stars, a gathering of mighty cosmic beings is established, part of a tradition which is nowhere written about but which was part of the inner history of the land long before Arthur, either as war-lord or king, was ever heard of. Known also as 'The Dwellers in Avalon', these archetypal figures send out a call which is answered in time by all who are drawn to study the Arthurian tradition. The power of the inner realms is thus conveyed, in a broad ray, outward from the centre, until it percolates through the worlds into the lands of men, where it works towards a cosmic goal hinted at in the mysteries of the Grail and in the deeds of the Round Table Fellowship. A word, whispered in Avalon, becomes a trumpet call in the ears of those who seek the good of the world and the furtherance of all mankind.

It is these things which make the Arthurian tradition such a powerful tool for the development of an inner reality capable of transcending time and space, a core of meaning from which it is possible to begin again the restoration of the world and those who dwell in it, until it once again shines forth in the starry firmament as it did of old.

But this can only happen if we will it, if the desire for good, for the healing of the wounded land and the wounded hearts of mankind, is strong enough to penetrate the darkness which obscures so much of the world at this time. Belief in, and practice of, the spiritual disciplines taught in the myths of the Grail, in the Cave of the Heart, and in the deeds of the Round Table Fellowship in the Lands Adventurous, can cause great and lasting changes in the world – perhaps beginning, in however small a way, the enormous tasks of restoring the Waste Lands, of healing the Wounded King, or of re-establishing the Logres within Britain in the hearts and minds of its people.

The myths of Arthur and the Round Table Fellowship embody this dream in tales of valour and chivalry, of quest and achievement. As the great Celticist Jean Markale put it:

> . . . many of the epic tales of war in the British and Irish traditions refer to symbolic conflicts. The symbols take various forms. We find brother fighting brother, hero against hero, gods against men and gods against fairy people. There are expeditions to the Other World, which may lie just around the corner or far over the water; and quests for mysterious objects which must be found for the hero to keep his strength or his honour. But all of them represent a concerted attempt to reconcile the contradictions inherent in social life and man's subsequent sense of alienation in its most profound diversity . . . Celtic epic portrays the great inner struggles of man and his conflicts with his environment through real battles against hostile forces.[49]

It was the struggle which gave rise to the Arthurian tradition. Through a study of its archetypal stories, we may begin to see ways in which the problems of our own time can be solved.

EXERCISE 7: THE ISLE OF DREAMS

The realms of faery lie just beyond sight at every turn in the road. We can find our way there through many different doors: through dream, through meditation, and through visiting the ancient places where the veils between the worlds are thinner than elsewhere. Once there, we should remember that it is a perilous place for mortals, who tend to go there and not return – or else to spend what seemed but a few moments, only to find that centuries have passed in the worlds above. Therefore we should observe certain rules, such as have come down to us from ancient traditions – not to eat of the food of Faery, nor drink aught but water; never to run widdershins (counter-clockwise) against the sun. And we should always obey the laws of the Otherworld, as they are presented to us when we walk there. With these thoughts in mind, we may go at will into the ancient realms, and come back again with more than Faery gold (such as turns to dust) in our possession.

You are standing on the threshold of the land, with a vast, grey-green expanse of sea stretching to the horizon before you. A ship of curious design approaches across the water. It is rowed by mermen, silver-scaled, with webbed fingers and strange, purple eyes. They show by signs that you should go aboard their craft, and you do so without hesitation, for you are assured that they mean you no harm. The boat begins to move at once, and you are soon crossing the limitless expanse of ocean at a swift pace. As they row the mermen set up a strange, wordless chant, which rises and falls to the rhythm of the oars.

Looking ahead you see an island rising from the sea, its tall cliffs ringed with towers and walls of unearthly design. The craft pulls in close against the cliffs, and you step ashore onto a beach of fine sand. From this, leading upward, is a spiralling path, which circles around the side of the island, climbing steadily, until it leads you onto the cliff-top. From there you look inland and see a castle which glimmers with a pale light, and you make your way towards it, knowing that here is your goal.

At the entrance to the castle you pause, looking in wonder at the high, smooth walls, decorated with fantastic images which are neither painted nor carved there, but which seem to be part of the stones themselves. Then the great gate opens, and a figure comes forth to greet you. She is a tall, beautiful woman, dressed in a flowing robe of green that seems like the sea itself. Her face seems rather cold at first but her eyes are brilliant and lustrous, and her greeting warm. She invites you to enter her realm and tells you her name: Morgain, Daughter of the Sea.

Within, the castle is as wondrous as it seemed from without. The walls gleam with nacerous lights, as though they were made of pearl, and everywhere are fantastic carvings depicting scenes of life in the magical realms of Faery such as are to be found in each of the elements – though here the sea is strongest. You follow the lady from room to room, growing ever more filled with wonder at all you see. Here are treasures beyond your wildest imagining, and objects of power and magic such as you have only read about.

Finally you reach a room near the heart of the castle – a beautiful room with couches of bronze and cedar-wood arranged in rows along either wall. Here the Lady Morgain stops and bids you take ease upon one of the couches. For here is the Chamber of Dreams, where you may lie for a while and learn the innermost secrets of your heart. Here you will dream true, and the images that arise will remain with you and become a part of you even when you depart from the island. Take your time now, and in this meditation see yourself lie down and close your inner eyes. Images will arise from the deepest levels of your consciousness, and you will have access to them again . . .

When you have dreamed and learned and awoken, refreshed, a silent merman is there to lead you again into the presence of the lady Morgain, whom you may now question, if you so desire, concerning anything you have seen. But remember that she is a great and powerful being, who must be treated with respect and forbearance. She can and will if she desires tell you much, including the mystery of her own role in the story of Arthur. For you have met and talked with the king already, and with Merlin who often came here before he withdrew to his own place. For this is but one of the many faces of Avalon, and if its ruler gives leave you may return to explore it further, meeting the ship on the same shoreline and sailing to land at other points around the island.

When the time seems right you should take your leave of the Lady of Avalon, and depart as you came, guided through the halls and passages of the castle by a silent merman, until you stand again on the cliff-top and see the boat lying at anchor below you. Descend the cliffs and go aboard; your journey home will be brief, and once you find yourself standing again on the point of the land, you should begin to return to everyday consciousness. But you will find that you are able to remember in great detail all that you saw, and especially the dream you had in the Hall of Dreams. When you are ready you may visit the island again, and learn more of the mysteries it holds in its secret heart.

8 · THE UNENDING SONG:

ARTHUR IN THE MODERN WORLD

Thus Arthur had himself borne to Avalon and he told his people that they should await him and he would return. And the Britons came back to Carduel and waited for him more than forty years before they would take a king, for they believed always that he would return. But this you know in truth that some have since then seen him hunting in the forest, and they have heard his dogs with him and some have hoped for a long time that he would return.

Didot Perceval

A MUTABLE IMAGE

From the start the Arthurian tradition has been subject to constant, often subtle degrees of change. The heroic mould which gave us the earliest figure of Arthur gave way to that of the chivalric king ruling over an elegant medieval court. Later ages presented a more political framework, with spurious prophecies, attributed to Merlin, declaring for the latest regime.

The Tudors in particular leant heavily on the existence of Arthur in their family tree to bolster their claims to the throne of Britain. Henry VII was extolled as 'The beast from North Wales, a man of renown . . . of the blood of Arthur . . . [Winner of] the great joy predicted by Merlin'. While Thomas Churchyard, in his book *The Worthiness of Wales* in 1587, referred to Elizabeth I as:

> She that sits in regall Throne,
> With Sceptre, Sword, and Crowne.
> (Who came from Arthur's rase and Iyne).

Still later, in 1610, the playwright Ben Jonson wrote a pageant called *The Speeches at Prince Henry's Barriers*, in which he described James I as the monarch who 'Wise, temperate, just, and stout, claims Arthur's seat', a reference no doubt to the then popular epigram which declared that:

> Charles James Steuart
> CLAIMES ARTHURS SEATE

On the literary horizon Arthur's star waned for a time. Spenser devoted the first part of his epic *The Faery Queen* to the deeds of young Prince Arthur, and clearly drew upon Malory and earlier sources for his inspiration. Merlin made a brief appearance in the story of *Don Quixote* by Miguel Cervantes. Milton contemplated an Arthurian epic but changed his mind in favour of the story of Adam and Eve. Later, the visionary poet and painter William Blake referred to Arthur and Merlin in some of his most important works.

Then in the nineteenth century came the birth of Romanticism, and with this the figures of Arthur, Guinevere, Lancelot and Tristan underwent a renaissance. The Poet Laureate, Alfred Tennyson, wrote a long series of 'idylls', poems whose sonorous rhythms brought back something of the original power of the romances – for all that Tennyson gave the knights Victorian values and all but dressed Arthur in a frock coat and stove-pipe hat!

Throughout the rest of the era Arthurian themes dominated the arts of poetry, music and painting. The Pre-Raphaelite Brotherhood, whose numbers included Edward Burne-Jones and William Morris, produced many striking pictures based on Arthurian themes; poetry, good, bad and indifferent, poured forth and was avidly read. The magic and beauty of the stories wove a spell over the drab Victorian age, touching again and again on the deepest levels of human experience.

Arthur Sailing to the Other World

A New Beginning

With the dawning of the twentieth century came war and destruction on a scale scarcely dreamed of before. A new breed of artist began to emerge, and among them were many who turned again to the images and stories of the Arthurian tradition for inspiration.

The poet and painter David Jones was one of these. He painted a number of extraordinary pictures on Arthurian themes – picturing the Grail Mass taking place in a bombed-out chapel in the middle of the new Waste Land of the Western Front. In his great poem In Parenthesis[28] he portrayed First World War soldiers fighting side by side with Arthurian heroes. And in the work which followed it, The Anathemata,[27] he produced an extraordinary evocation of Britain from its geological past to a semi-mythic eternity, bringing in the themes of Arthur and the Grail with tremendous force and vitality.

Modern techniques of archaeology, and further research into the sparse documents of the sixth and seventh centuries, began to reveal more of the reality behind the earliest heroic tales. The so-called Dark Ages were no longer so opaque, and with this ever-widening pool of knowledge to draw upon, once again novelists and poets drew on the Arthurian tradition for their inspiration.

A number of memorable historical novels appeared from the 1940s onwards. Edward Frankland wrote a detailed and poetic account of the historical Arthur in his book The Bear of Britain,[16] and this was followed by such works as The Great Captains by Henry Treece,[85] which told the story from the viewpoint of Mordred; Porius by John Cowper Powys[66] – a vast sprawling romance worthy of the best of its medieval forbears but wholly contemporary; and perhaps best of all The Sword at Sunset by Rosemary Sutcliff,[80] which evoked a totally human Arthur, touched with the magic of a forgotten age, tragic and noble, still striving towards the ideal kingdom of Malory's Le Morte D'Arthur and the writers of The Vulgate Cycle.

T.H. White published a quartet of books under the overall title The Once and Future King,[90] taking the Latin epitaph said to be carved upon the tomb where Arthur's bones had never lain. In this he set out to retell the story as Malory had given it, but with certain significant changes. The first book, The Sword in the Stone, tells the story of Arthur's childhood and training at the hands of Merlin – or rather, as White spells it, Merlyn. This rather comical old gentleman, who lives backwards and is thus enabled to see the future which, to him, has already happened, seems a far cry from the Merlin of earlier times. Yet his magic is no less potent. Arthur learns the things which he needs to fit him for the great task ahead by taking the shapes of bird, beast and insect, each of which shows him the foolishness of the ways of men.

But this light-hearted beginning becomes gradually darkened in the books which follow. The Queen of Air and Darkness concentrates on the figure of Morgause, and the childhood of her sons Gawain, Gareth, Gaheries and Agravaine, and culminates in the birth of Mordred, whose coming is to spell destruction for the Arthurian world. The third book, The Ill-Made Knight, tells the story of Lancelot and Guinevere with a degree of passion and psychological realism seldom attained before or since. Finally, The Candle in the Wind tells the story of the downfall of the Round Table, the war against Lancelot and the doom-laden end to the tale. A fifth volume, left unfinished by White at his death, was published later as The Story of Merlyn.[91] It tells what happens when the old wizard returns to Arthur's tent on the eve of the battle of Camlan, as he takes his protégé through a further series of transformations which equip him for a new beginning after his time in Avalon. It is marred by White's bitter response to the imminent war with Germany, but it nevertheless contains some of his finest writing, taking Arthur on beyond the darkness in which his dream ends, towards a new source of light.

Poets also did not neglect the tradition. Another Poet Laureate, John Masefield, produced a series of powerful lyrics in Midsummer Night,[51] mingling the heroic and the romantic elements of the old stories in a wholly new way. Charles Williams, one of the august group known as the Inklings, who included J.R.R. Tolkien and C.S. Lewis among their number, wrote what is still the most powerful and magical series of poems on the theme of the Grail, creating an entire world, stretching from the negative realm of P'o L'u, the realm of negative evil, to the great city of the Grail at Sarras. No simple account can give any real idea of the magisterial quality of these poems, which appeared in two volumes, Taliesin through Logres and The Region of the Summer Stars[92]. The following gives only a taste, which should be supplemented by a reading of all the works, together with the forthcoming book by Gareth Knight.[33]

Here Merlin and his twin sister Brisen, who stand for Time and Space in Williams' universe, and are the daughters of Nimue (Nature) enact a magical operation to assist in the founding of the Arthurian kingdom.

> The cone's shadow of earth fell into space,
> and into (other than space) the third heaven.
> In the third heaven are the living unriven truths,
> climax tranquil in Venus. Merlin and Brisen
> heard, as in faint bee-like humming
> round the cone's point, the feeling intellect hasten
> to fasten on the earth's image; in the third heaven
> the stones of the waste glimmered like summer stars.
> Between wood and waste the yoked children of Nimue
> opened the rite; they invoked the third heaven,

> heard in the far humming of the spiritual intellect,
> to the building of Logres and the coming of the land of the Trinity
> which is called Sarras in maps of the soul. Merlin
> made preparation; . . .
> He lifted the five times cross-incised rod
> and began incantation; in the tongue of Broceliande
> adjuring all the primal atoms of earth
> to shape the borders of Logres, to the dispensation
> of Carbonek to Caerleon, of Caerleon to Camelot, to the union
> of King Pelles and King Arthur . . .

Another distinguished poet, John Heath Stubbs, gave his vision of Arthur in a wide-ranging epic entitled *Artorious*,[24] combining myth, romance, and the heroic in a subtle blend. More recently still there has been a positive spate of novels: *Mists of Avalon* by Marion Zimmer Bradley;[4] *Down the Long Wind* by Gillian Bradshaw, a trilogy of novels on Merlin by Mary Stewart,[72, 73, 74] and another by Stephen Lawhead, *Taliesin, Merlin,* and *Arthur*.[38, 39, 40] Each of these last-named works has introduced a powerful strain of magic into its retelling of the stories, thus widening and deepening their application to the contemporary seeker. Bradley tells her story from the viewpoint of Morgan le Fay, evoking a rich vision of Avalon as a Faery world which is gradually floating further away from the historical realm of Arthur. The same author also invokes the shadow of Atlantis in the early part of the book, taking up an idea first put forward in a received text by Dion Fortune, that Arthur's mother Igrain was one of the few who escaped (along with Merlin) from the drowned continent – bringing with her the blood-line and magical knowledge of the most ancient and advanced civilisation on earth.

Stephen Lawhead expands on this still further by making the survivors of the cataclysm found various communities at Glastonbury and elsewhere in Britain – foundations which become synonymous in the minds of the original inhabitants with the *Sidhe*.

Gillian Bradshaw, in her series of books about Gawain, again introduces magical themes into the narrative, giving to her hero the task of finding and wielding the magical sword of light under the aegis of the god Lugh. In doing so she harks back to a tradition which makes Gawain the wielder of Excalibur, gifted to him by Arthur for a time in the wars against the Saxons.

Merlin, in Mary Stewart's trilogy, is more of a modern magician than the inspired druid of earlier texts. Yet he is a recognisable descendant of the Merlin Ambrosius written about by Geoffrey of Monmouth – falling into inspired trances, and suffering the terrible agonies of the gifted psychic who sees all but is helpless to do more than watch as the kingdom he helped to create falls back into the darkness from which it emerged.

Contemporary cinema likewise has not neglected the realms of Arthur. At least one recent work, *Excalibur*, directed by John Boorman, and co-written with Rospo Pallenburg, gives a marvellously rich account of the whole cycle from Arthur's birth to the Last Battle. Though compressed at times to a point where it is difficult to comprehend, the sub-text of the film has a unity rare in any Arthurian work. It makes significant use of the symbolism of the Grail quest, and successfully demonstrates the links between Arthur and the Wounded King, who in this version are one. It also contains the best portrayal of Merlin to date, as a wise, quirky, sorrowful figure who is the last Dragon Priest of Britain and draws upon the immense power of the inner earth to bring about his magical operations.

A MAGICAL DIMENSION

Such operations are by no means confined to works of fiction or to the cinema screen. A common factor in many of the modern works discussed here is their inclusion not only of historical and mythic elements of the stories, but also of their magical and esoteric significance. Thus Diana Paxson in her novel of Tristan, *The White Raven*,[65] draws upon her own knowledge of magic as a priestess of the Covenant of the Goddess; while the magical descriptions contained in Charles Williams' writings draw upon his own years in the Magical Order of the Golden Dawn.

As long ago as the 1890s this prestigious group, which included A.E. Waite, W.B. Yeats and (briefly) Aleister Crowley among its numbers, were drawing upon the Arthurian tradition in their magical operations; work which was continued by Dion Fortune in the Society of the Inner Light,[15] and thereafter by the Servants of the Light School of Quabalistic Science, and by individuals such as Gareth Knight, R.J. Stewart and the present writer.

It is part of the ultimate value and importance of the Arthurian tradition that, because it is founded upon esoteric principles, embodying such many and varied archetypal forces, it is unusually apposite for magical work. An example of this to which the present author was witness took place during a weekend workshop in Gloucestershire in 1982. In this, a tremendous pool of energy was built up, using the group consciousness of the fifty to sixty people present. When this had been allowed to create its own vortex of power, the operator leading the group proceeded to 'summon' Arthur, Guinevere, Merlin and Morgan back from tthe inner realms. The immediacy and power of the response was total. The Arthurian archetypes were quite literally present among the group, and remained so for some time after. In a certain sense the Sleeping Lord was recalled from Avalon, and sent forth again into the world to work for the restoration of the kingdom. Later, in several further operations carried out by the same group and its offshoots, this work was continued and strrengthened, at actual sites with Arthurian associations, at further group meetings and by individuals working alone.

Another first-hand account adds further details:

> The prophecy of the return of Arthur was fulfilled that night at the Camelot we had built; after a reading of Tennyson's *Morte d'Arthur* we invited back into our company the redeemed archetypes of the Round Table. We sat silently, for what seemed an age, invoking the personages with whom we had become so familiar throughout the weekend, sending them forth to intercede with the troubled world of our own times and inviting in those of our friends and family who might wish to share in our fellowship. It was truly an awesome and splendid thing that we did. The power which we invoked was both visible and perceptible in every sense: the candles on the altar shimmering with a radiance greater than their own. None of us wanted to leave: we were gripped, not by fear, but by a longing to remain. Then one by one the company dispersed to bear into the world the substance of what we had experienced, to continue the work of the Round Table within our own sphere of life.[55]

This operation culminated for the present (though by no means for ever) in a large-scale working in 1987, intended to bring about the Restoration of the Courts of Joy, the deeply magical place in which the four Hallows of the Grail myth, Cup, Spear, Stone and Sword, were set once more at power-points in the body of Logres – there to work actively for the healing of the land and those who dwell upon it.[56]

Such accounts as that given above can in no wise substitute for an active participation in the Arthurian mysteries, of which this book has attempted to give a brief account. First-hand experience of the archetypal forces can only be had by working with them, and various methods of so doing are given throughout these pages.

There are many other valid systems with which to work, and the present author does not wish to denigrate any by concentrating on the Arthurian tradition, which, though it is grounded in our native soil, has become universal through its wider application. No matter in what part of the world those who wish to explore it may live, the same values still obtain. The heart legends of many lands, from Africa to Russia, have their own Arthurs, their own Merlins, their own rich heritage of traditions which draw upon the same basic source.

In this country the enduring fame and magical potency of Arthur continues to burn with a steady flame. The traditions which speak of him as the Sleeping Lord, the tutelary spirit of inner Britain, embody a reality of great power. The poet David Jones, already referred to, summed this up in a work which itself bore the title *The Sleeping Lord*.[29] One passage seems particularly appropriate to end with, before we go on to the final exercise and a new vision of the Arthurian tradition.

> how long has he been the sleeping lord?
> are the clammy ferns
>
>   his rustling vallance
> does the buried rowan
>
>   ward him from evil, or
> does he ward the tanglewood
>
>   and the denizens of the wood
> are the stunted oaks his gnarled guard
>
>   or are their knarred limbs
> strong with his sap? . . .
> Does the land wait the sleeping lord
>
>   or is the wasted land
> that very lord who sleeps?

EXERCISE 8: THE FUTURE KING

Arthur is called the Once and Future King because he is an aspect of an archetype which spans eternity. He has been part of the history of this world for nearly as long as it has existed – not as Arthur of Britain, but as earlier figures who became, finally, embodied in the figure of the part-historical, part-mythical hero. When the time came for this figure to depart, it was not fitting that he should die. 'Not wise the thought, a grave for Arthur' runs an old Welsh poem. Instead he withdrew, like Merlin before him, into a hidden place, where he is portrayed as sleeping until the day arrives when he is summoned back to continue the work he began long ago. Whether or not one chooses to believe that this calling has already been made (see Chapter 8), there is that in Arthur which never sleeps, which can be contacted as we did in the very first exercise in this book. The time has come now, having worked through the various degrees of awareness presented in the exercises, to return to the inner place of the Sleeping Lord, and there to offer him what we have learned.

Preparing, then, for meditation, you sink deeply into the very stuff of the land, feeling the living earth, most dense of elements, upon all sides, yet passing unharmed through it until you emerge in a great cavern, far below the surface of the land. It is lit by a light which seems to come from the walls, and by that light you perceive a great stone bed in the centre of the cavern, on which is laid the figure of the man, far greater in size than any mortal. He lies upon one side, knees drawn up a little, one hand pillowing his head. His hair and beard are as brown as when he first lay down to his long sleep, many centuries ago, and there is a sense of peace about him which belies the warlike appearance of the great sword which lies at his side, the shield propped against the bed, the spear laid upon the ground ready to be picked up in a moment, and the fine cote of mail which hangs close by.

This is both like and unlike the figure you met earlier – there is the same look of nobility and inner strength about him, tempered by sorrow; but this is an aspect whose dimensions are in every way greater: not only is the Sleeping Lord of vaster proportions, so too are the strengths and abilities you sense within him.

As you stand by you become aware that the eyes of the great figure are open, and that he is regarding you with warmth and friendliness tempered by curiosity. He does not move, yet you sense a probing intelligence reaching out to you, reading what is to be read within the book of your life. You may feel shame or exultation at this, according to your nature.

Then, though no word is spoken, you feel yourself lifted up, passing like an insubstantial dream through the earth, outward and upward into the heavens. From here, looking down, you can see a part of the land beneath which you recently stood. And you see that this land is the figure of the King: his limbs forming the hills and valleys, his body the green mound beneath which he also sleeps. And looking outward from where you now stand, you see that, mirrored among the stars, is yet another form, vaster even than the one below, a vast network of energies, coupling worlds and even solar systems together.

You turn away in awe, for this is the Cosmic King, of whom the Sleeping Lord and the Warrior Arthur are but shadows. You close your inner eyes and in a moment find yourself back again in the cavern, looking into the calm gaze of the sleeper who has awoken. The time has come to make your offering, which is of all that you have learned and understood in your journeys to the inner realms, all that is your part of the tradition, the ongoing story which has no end yet dreamed of by men . . .

When you have made your affirmation, and when it has been received, you begin to return, floating upwards through the thick darkness of the earth until you emerge once more in the place from which you began this meditation. Regard this if you will as the seal upon all work that is done by you hereafter within this sphere of understanding. For what Arthur has received others are aware of, and because of it you are blessed by the Dwellers in Avalon.

May you continue to find ever-greater riches and ever-deepening wisdom in the lands of Arthur.

Glossary of
Arthurian
Characters

Agravain: son of *Lot* and *Morgause*, the third of the Orkney brothers, who included *Gawain*, *Gaheries* and *Gareth*. Less reliable than the others, Agravain was involved in the plot against *Lancelot* which brought down the chivalry of the Round Table. He met his death at the hands of Lancelot in the fighting outside the queen's chamber.

Ambrosius Aurelianus: *Vortigern's* successor and brother of *Uther*.

Arthur: son of *Uther* and *Igrain*. It was said that his mother had been among those who escaped from Atlantis before the great continent sank. Others maintained that she had faery blood. Certainly Uther possessed the ancient blood of the British kings, being descended from a line of rulers. Arthur became the sacred king of Britain on drawing a sword from a stone – not Excalibur as is sometimes believed, but a symbol of his right to rule arranged by *Merlin*, who had brought about his birth by disguising Uther to look like Igrain's husband *Gorlois*, and who afterwards became his adviser.

Bedevere: Knight of the Round Table. One of the first to join the

Fellowship, he become the Butler to the court, organising feasts and tournaments along with the irascible *Kay*. A warrior in his own right, he was with Arthur to the end and finally threw the enchanted sword Excalibur back into the lake from which it had come.

Bertilak: Knight transformed, by *Morgan*, into the likeness of the Green Knight. He stands for the principle of winter, and is, in his alternate guise, a vegetation god whose task it is to test and then initiate Gawain into the mysteries of the Goddess. Lady Bercilak, his wife, was forced to attempt the seduction of *Gawain* so that he would betray the vows of chivalry and thus damage the reputation of the Round Table. At a deeper level she is one of the aspects of the Goddess whose tempting role was also designed to initiate Gawain into her service.

Blaise: the master of *Merlin* to whom, in the *Didot Perceval*,[70] he makes his report before retiring. A shadowy figure, described as a monk or hermit in most texts, but in reality suggesting a more ancient and primal figure who taught Merlin the secret arts.

Bors: cousin of *Lancelot*. One of the strongest knights of the Round Table, he became the third of the trio of successful Grail Knights. Steadiness and dependability were his chief aspects. He alone returned to Camelot at the end of the great quest to tell *Arthur* and the rest what had occurred. Later he refused to defend *Guinevere* against accusations of adultery, changed his mind and then was relieved by Lancelot, who appeared at the last moment to save her. Surviving most of the Fellowship, he died in Palestine fighting in the Crusades.

Bran: ancestral King of Britain, one of the powerful titanic gods who ruled the land before the coming of *Arthur*. He also prefigures the Wounded King of the later stories. At his death he commanded that his head be cut off and carried to the island of Gwales where it continued to oraculate for many years until one of the company who accompanied it opened a forbidden door, at which point the head fell silent and began to decay. It was then carried to the White Mount in London and buried there in accordance with Bran's wishes, so that he might continue to defend the country against invasion. Arthur later ordered the head dug up so that he alone was considered the defender of Britain.

Brangaine: the companion of *Isolt of Cornwall* who gives *Tristan* and her mistress the love potion brewed by Isolt's mother intended for the wedding night of Isolt with Mark. After Tristan becomes the lover of her mistress she agrees to substitute herself on the wedding night so that Mark will never know that his wife was no longer a virgin.

Brisen: the nurse of *Elaine of Corbenic*. It is she who arranges the deception by which *Galahad* is engendered, giving *Lancelot* a drugged drink which causes him to believe that he is with *Guinevere*. Waking to discover that it is Elaine beside him in bed Lancelot almost kills her, then runs mad for a time. Elaine brings up Galahad then sends him to the care of nuns at Amesbury.

Culhwch: early Celtic hero whose quest for Olwen White-Footprint, daughter of Yspadadden Chief-Giant, lead him to request aid from his cousin *Arthur*. A fantastic collection of heroes with Otherworldly abilities are dispatched to help the youth, and a mass of fragmentary hero tales are drawn upon for the adventures that follow.

Dagonet: *Arthur's* court jester who became a Knight of the Round Table and whose gentle mockery made him among the most popular figures in the Arthurian panoply. He became an especial friend of *Tristan*, more than once rescuing him from capture by *Mark*.

Dindraine: the sister of *Perceval*, who accompanies the Grail Knights and eventually sacrifices herself in order to heal a leprous woman. Her body is carried in the magical Ship of Solomon to the sacred city of Sarras, where it is buried alongside that of *Galahad*. As the only woman involved in the Grail quest, her role is of the utmost importance. She represents, along with *Elaine of Corbenic*, the feminine mysteries of the Grail.

Ector: the foster-father of *Arthur*. He brought up the young king in ignorance of his identity after being entrusted with the child by *Merlin*.

Elaine of Astolat: the maiden by whose father *Lancelot* is secretly armed for a tournament. She falls in love with the famous knight and when she realises that he will never return that love, she starves herself to death. Her body is put into a boat and carried down river to Camelot where all are saddened by her fate.

Elaine of Corbenic: the daughter of *Pelles*, of the Grail Family. *Brisen* gives *Lancelot* a drugged potion so that he believes he is sleeping with *Guinevere*. When he discovers the deception he goes mad for a time, but is finally discovered and healed by Elaine.

She fades rather from the scene at this junction, but features as the Grail Princess under other names in the rest of the Arthurian sagas.

Gaheries: son of *Lot* and *Morgause*. The second of the Orkney brothers, he discovers that Morgause has taken the knight *Lamorack* as her lover, and discovering them in bed together cuts off his mother's head in a fit of passion. He later dies at *Lancelot*'s hand in the battle to rescue *Guinevere* from the stake.

Galahad: son of *Elaine of Corbenic* and *Lancelot*. He surpasses his father in both chivalry and purity of life, becoming the achiever of the Grail along with *Perceval* and *Bors*. His relationship with his father is touching and enlightening, and his last words are to tell Bors to 'remember me to my father Sir Lancelot'.

Galahaut the Haut Prince: Lord of the Kingdom of Surluse. He wars against *Arthur* in the early days of the young king's reign, but finally surrenders after observing the chivalry of *Lancelot*, whose devoted follower he then becomes. Finally, believing Lancelot dead, he refuses to eat and starves himself to death. He is buried with honour at Lancelot's castle of Joyous Gard.

Gareth of Orkney: third son of *Lot* and *Morgause*, he comes anonymously to court and is called Beaumains (Fair Hands) by *Kay*, who puts him to work in the kitchens. He requests that he be allowed to go on the adventure of *Linet* and distinguishes himself greatly, fighting a series of multi-coloured knights. He is knighted by *Lancelot* whose devoted follower he becomes, and is tragically slain by the great knight during the battle to rescue *Guinevere* from the stake.

Gawain: son of *King Lot of Orkney*. The eldest of the Orkney brothers, he was the greatest knight at the Arthurian court until the coming of *Lancelot*. His reputation suffered due to his allegiance to the Goddess, whose champion and lover he became after the initiation tests of the Green Knight, and his marriage to *Ragnall*. The death of his brothers at Lancelot's hands drove him to become the bitterest foe of his once greatest friend. He died at last, from wounds received in a fight that Lancelot never wished for. His ghost appeared to *Arthur* before the battle of Camlan.

Gorlois: Duke of Cornwall, first husband of *Igrain*. He fights a bitter war with *Uther* and is finally slain in a foray from the castle of Tintagel. *Merlin* then disguises Uther so that he has the appearance of Gorlois, in which form he engenders *Arthur* upon Igrain, whom he later marries.

Gromer Somer Joure: brother of *Ragnall* who challenges *Arthur* with a riddle: 'What is it women most desire?'. A powerful Otherworldly figure and enchanter, he is defeated by Arthur with the help of *Gawain* and confesses that he was himself enchanted by *Morgan le Fay*.

Guinevere: daughter of Leodegrance and wife of *Arthur*. Her affair with *Lancelot* brings down the kingdom, and she ends her days in the nunnery of Amesbury, where she is finally buried after taking a last leave of Lancelot. Her original role was as the Flower Bride, an ancient aspect of the Goddess whose function was to be fought over by the contending powers of summer and winter. At one time Arthur and Lancelot must have taken these roles.

Igrain: mother of *Arthur*. Tradition speaks of her as coming from Atlantis, but in most versions of the story she is the wife of *Gorlois* of Cornwall, with whom *Uther* falls in love, and through *Merlin*'s enchantment is given the likeness of Igrain's husband so that Uther can beget Arthur upon her.

Isolt of Cornwall: daughter of King Anguish of Ireland. She was the intended wife of *Mark of Cornwall*, but became the lover of *Tristan* after drinking a love potion intended for her wedding night. A famous beauty, her affair with Tristan shocked the Arthurian court and drew attention for a time from the love of *Lancelot* and *Guinevere*. Arriving too late to save Tristan from a poisoned wound, she fell dead and was buried alongside him in Brittany.

Isolt of the White Hands: daughter of the King of Brittany, she became *Tristan*'s wife at the behest of her brother Kaherdin. The marriage was not consummated and Isolt became bitter towards her husband – finally bringing about his death by lying about the colour of the sails on the ship bringing *Isolt of Ireland* to his aid. She committed suicide shortly after.

Joseph of Arimathaea: saint. A rich Jew with connections in the Cornish tin trade, he may have visited Britain with the young Jesus. Later, after the Crucifixion, he claimed the body of the Messiah and interred it in his own tomb. As a reward he was later given custodianship of the Grail and founded a family of guardians who continued to watch over it until the time of its achieving by *Galahad*, who was a direct descendent of Joseph. He is also credited with building the first Christian church, dedicated to the Virgin Mary, at Glastonbury in Somerset.

Kay: *Arthur*'s foster-brother, son of *Ector*. He became Arthur's Seneschal, and served him faithfully in this office until the end of the Round Table. His irascible nature and occasional cruelty earned him an unsympathetic reputation, but he was a good knight for all that and seems to have been genuinely loved by Arthur.

Lamorack: son of *Pellinore*. One of the strongest Knights of the Round Table, he fell in love with *Morgause* and was finally murdered by *Gawain* and his brothers after *Gaheries* had himself cut off his mother's head when he found her in bed with Lamorack.

Lancelot: son of King Ban of Benwick, sometimes called Lancelot du Lac, after his fostering in the Otherworldly realm of the Lake. He retained many qualities of the faery knight, which enabled him to take his place as the most renowned of *Arthur*'s knights. He took over from *Gawain* the role of queen's champion, and so fell in love with *Guinevere*. There are many stories which tell of Lancelot's prowess and his attempts to rid the kingdom of evil custom: in this guardianship of the land, he substitutes the kingly role of Arthur. After being tricked into sleeping with *Elaine of Corbenic* he ran mad. After his healing, he took part in the Grail quest. Unable to attain the vessel himself, due to his adulterous love of Guinevere, he is none the less represented and surpassed by *Galahad* his son. Eventually banished from court, he became a hermit after Arthur's passing.

Lot: King of Orkney and husband of *Morgause*. At the beginning of *Arthur*'s reign, he was one of the rebel kings. The Orkney clan, consisting of his sons *Gawain*, *Agravain*, *Gaheries* and *Gareth* and their mother retain some animosity towards Arthur's reign; though, ironically, it is in *Mordred*, the son of Morgause by Arthur, that the seeds of former rebellion surface. He was killed by *Pellinore*.

Linet: sometimes called Le Demoiselle Sauvage. Linet comes to court asking help for her imprisoned sister, *Lionors*. The only available knight is the recently knighted Beaumains – *Gareth* – whose chivalric inexperience she unmercifully taunts. She also appears in an earlier story as the guide and protector of *Owein*.

Lionors: sister of *Linet*. She is rescued by *Gareth* who later marries her.

Mark: King of Cornwall, uncle of *Tristan* whom he sends to obtain his bride, *Isolt*, daughter of the King of Ireland, with disastrous results for his own happiness. Isolt avoids her own wedding night by sending her companion, *Brangaine*, to Mark's bed. Mark is represented as a cuckold who condones Isolt's infidelity, though he frequently pursued the queen and his nephew.

Merlin: magician and guardian of the Pendragon line. Born to a virgin who was visited by a spirit, Merlin Emrys was discovered by Vortigern's men as the perfect sacrifice to help seal the foundations of his tumbling-down tower. Merlin tells of the eternal battle between the dragons which underlie the foundations in a story which reflects the racial nature of this theme. He makes prophecies about Britain in gnomic verses and becomes the adviser of *Ambrosius Aurelianus* and his brother *Uther*, in the course of whose reign he magically builds Stonehenge. Arthur inherits Merlin as magical adviser for only a short while, before Merlin returns to his father's realm to become the eternal guardian of Britain, according to earlier sources, or succumbs to the charms of *Nimue*, according to later French sources. Merlin is the chief architect of the Pendragons' strategy and the inner guardian of the land which, in early times, was called *Clas Merddin* or Merlin's Enclosure.

Mordred: the incestuously begotten son of Arthur and *Morgause*. When Arthur realised that he had slept with his half-sister, he attempted to kill his son by issuing a Herod-like proclamation that all babies born at that time be exposed in an open boat. Mordred survived to be raised by Morgause who eventually sent him to court, though Mordred was never openly recognised as Arthur's son or successor. When the Round Table was in collapse, Mordred capitalised on the weakness of the realm and Arthur's absence to seize command. He was slain by Arthur, whom he mortally wounded.

Morgan le Fay: daughter of *Gorlois* and *Igrain*. She was sent to a monastery, ostensibly to be educated as a nun, though she learned the magical arts. She made a political match with *Uriens of Gore* and became the mother of *Owein*. Ever at enmity with *Arthur* and his plans, she seemed to be ever plotting some new enormity. However, Morgan's role as protector of the land led her to adopt some challenging measures to keep Arthur's kingship bright. Morgan has many early and Celtic correlatives which make plain the nature of her role as guardian of Britain's sovereignty, which she in many ways embodies.

Morgause: wife of *Lot*, daughter of *Igrain* and *Gorlois*. She was politically married to *Lot of Orkney*, by whom she had *Gawain*, *Gaheries*, *Agravain* and *Gareth*. She bore *Mordred* to *Arthur* after having seduced her half-brother on the eve of his coronation. She became *Lamorack*'s mistress and, on being discovered in bed with him, was slain by Gaheries.

Morold: *Isolt of Cornwall*'s uncle, sometimes called Marhaus. *Mark* had to pay a levy to *Anguish of Ireland*; when he discontinued this payment, Morold was sent out to fight Mark's champion *Tristan*, whom he wounded severely and by whom he was slain.

Nimue: sometimes also called Vivianne. She was the daughter of Dionas, a gentleman who was a votary of Diana. Nimue was conflated with the Lady of the Lake in later traditions. *Merlin* taught her magic, and eventually became infatuated with her, according to Malory, so that Nimue was able to entice and imprison him under a great stone. She then adopted Merlin's magical mantle throughout the rest of the story.

Owein: son of *Morgan* and *Uriens*, sometimes called Ywain. Owein is one of the earliest Arthurian knights and, in the *Mabinogion*, becomes the husband of the Lady of the Fountain and the master of the Enchanted Games. In later tradition, Owein prevents Morgan from killing his father. He also rescues a lion which becomes his companion, by which he is sometimes also called the Knight of the Lion.

Palomides: Saracen knight, in love with *Isolt of Cornwall*. He became the pursuer of the Questing Beast, after the death of *Pellinore*.

Pelles: King of Corbenic and member of the Grail Family. Also called Pellam. Pelles was wounded with the Dolorous Spear by Balin and so became the King of the Waste Land, which could not be restored save by the Grail winner. Pelles condoned the use of magic to lure *Lancelot* to sleep with his daughter, *Elaine of Corbenic*, in order that this achiever of the Grail could be engendered.

Pellinore: King Pellinore was the father of *Perceval* and *Lamorack*. His chief task was the pursuit of the Questing Beast. Because Pellinore had killed *Lot*, a long feud lay between the families of Pellinore and Orkney. Eventually *Gawain* and *Gaheries* slew Pellinore in revenge.

Perceval: son of *Pellinore*, one of the Grail winners. According to most traditions, Perceval was raised by his mother in ignorance of arms and courtesy, but his natural prowess led him to *Arthur*'s court where he immediately set off in pursuit of a knight who had insulted *Guinevere*. His further training in arms brought him into the hall of the Fisher King where he forbore to ask the all-healing Grail Question out of ill-placed courtesy. His subsequent quest and finding of the Grail is related in the earlier traditions, where he becomes the new Grail Guardian. However, later texts replace Perceval by *Galahad* as the Grail winner. Perceval there becomes Galahad's companion. Perceval's early ignorance has tagged him 'the Perfect Fool', but his is a Christ-like simplicity without offence which matures into real insight and wisdom.

Ragnall: sister of *Gromer*. Enchanted into the shape of an ugly hag by *Morgan*, she comes to the rescue of *Arthur* who strives to find the answer to Gromer's riddle. She agrees to tell him the answer in return for her marriage to *Gawain*. Arthur trustfully accepts on Gawain's behalf. Gromer arrives and poses the question once more: 'What is it women most desire?' and Arthur relates the answer: 'Women desire to have sovereignty over men.' Gawain and Ragnall are wed and, at their first kiss, she is transformed into a beautiful maiden. However, Gawain is asked to decide whether she shall be fair by day and foul by night, or the reverse. Fully realising the meaning of the riddle, Gawain begs her to choose and Ragnall is forever disenchanted.

Tristan: *Mark*'s nephew, lover of *Isolt of Cornwall*. Sent by Mark to fetch his bride, Tristan falls in love with Isolt by means of drinking the love potion. Their chequered love is marked by continual pursuits by Mark, near-escapes and subterfuges. After being healed by her of a poisoned arrow wound, Tristan marries another Isolt, *Isolt of the White Hands*, with whom he is unable to find happiness. Tristan dies without seeing his former Isolt. Tristan is the truly bardic knight, without the pristine chivalry of *Lancelot:* a true Celt in his poetic love-making.

Uriens of Gore: one of the early rebels against *Arthur*, he remained one of Arthur's most faithful fellowers. He was father of *Owein* and husband of *Morgan*.

Uther Pendragon: father of *Arthur*, second husband of *Igrain*. After becoming king, Uther saw Igrain and lusted for her. He lay siege to her husband, *Gorlois'*, castle and, in his absence, and with the aid of *Merlin*, took on the shape of Gorlois in order to sleep with her. In the same hour Gorlois perished in battle. Uther retains the earliest resonances of the Arthurian legend, the bedrock upon which they are established; his taking of Igrain for himself, coupled with further hints in other texts, reveals him to have practised 'the Custom of the Pendragon' – a form of *droit du seigneur* with the women of his realm.

Vortigern: the predecessor of *Ambrosius*, who invited Saxon mercenaries into Britain in order to protect the realm: an action hardly popular among the people. His attempts to build a tower stronghold came to nothing, for it kept tumbling down. Counselled by this druids to sacrifice a boy without a father, Vortigern found *Merlin* who challenged his druids and then prophesied the fate of Britain. Vortigern died shortly after.

BIBLIOGRAPHY

(unless otherwise stated all titles are published in London)

1. ANDREAS CAPELLANUS *The Art of Courtly Love*, trans. J.J. Parry, New York, Norton & Co.,1969.
2. ASHE, G. 'Merlin in the Earliest Records', in *The Book of Merlin*, ed. R.J. Stewart, Poole, Blandford Press, 1987.
3. BEROUL, *The Romance of Tristan*, trans. A.S. Frederick, Penguin Books, 1970.
4. BRADLEY, M.Z., *The Mists of Avalon*, Michael Joseph, 1983.
5. BRADSHAW, G., *Down the Long Wind*, Methuen, 1988.
6. BROMWICH, R., *Trioedd Ynys Prydein*, Cardiff, University of Wales Press, 1978.
7. CHAMBERS, A.K., *Arthur of Britain*, Sidgewick & Jackson, 1927.
8. CHRETIEN DE TROYES, *Arthurian Romances*, trans. D.D.R. Owen, Dent, 1987.
9. *Le Chevalier de Papegau*, ed. & trans. T.E. Vesce, New York, Garland Publishing, 1986.
10. CROSS, T.P. & SLOVER, C.H., *Ancient Irish Tales*, Dublin Figgis, 1936.
11. DANTE ALIGHIERI, *The Divine Comedy*, trans Lawrence Binyon, Agenda Editions, 1979.
12. DE ROUGEMONT, D., *Love in the Western World*, New York, Pantheon, 1969.

13. EISNER, S., *The Tristan Legend*, Illinois, Northwestern University Press, 1969.
14. EVANS, S., *In Quest of the Holy Grail*, J.M. Dent, 1898.
15. FORTUNE, D., *Avalon of the Heart*, Wellingborough, Aquarian Press, 1971.
16. FRANKLAND, E., *The Bear of Britain*, Macdonald, 1941.
17. FRANZ, M.-L. *C.G. Jung: His Myth in Our Time*, Hodder & Stoughton, 1975.
18. GARDNER, J., *The Complete Works of the Gawain Poet*, Southern Illinois University Press, 1965.
19. GASTER, M., 'The Legend of Merlin', *Folklore* 16 (1905).
20. GEOFFREY OF MONMOUTH *The History of the Kings of Britain*, trans. Lewis Thorpe, Penguin, 1966.
21. GEOFFREY OF MONMOUTH, *The Vita Merlini*, trans. J.J. Parry, University of Illinois, 1925.
22. GOTTFRIED VON STRASSBOURG, *Tristan*, trans. A.T. Hatto, Penguin Books, 1967.
23. HALL, L.B., *The Knightly Tales of Sir Gawain*, Chicago, Ill., Nelson Hall, 1976.
24. HEATH-STUBBS, J., *Artorius*, Enitharmon Press, 1974.
25. JOHNSON, R.A., *The Psychology of Romantic Love*, Routledge & Kegan Paul, 1983.
26. JONES, D.E.F., *The English Spirit*, Rudolf Steiner Press, 1982.
27. JONES, D., *The Anathemata*, Faber, 1952.
28. JONES, D., *In Parenthesis*, Faber, 1937
29. JONES, D., *The Sleeping Lord*, Faber, 1974.
30. KARR. P.A., *The King Arthur Companion*, Albany, Chaosium Inc., 1983.
31. KENNEDY, B., *Knighthood in the Morte Darthur*, Cambridge, D.S. Brewer, 1986.
32. KNIGHT, G., 'The Archetype of Merlin', in *The Book of Merlin*, ed. R.J. Stewart, Poole, Blandford Press, 1987.
33. KNIGHT, G., *The Magical World of the Inklings*, Shaftesbury, Element Books, forthcoming, 1991.
34. KNIGHT, G., *The Secret Tradition in Arthurian Legend*, Wellingborough, Aquarian Press, 1983.
35. LACY, N.J. & ASHE, G., *The Arthurian Handbook*, New York, Garland Publishing Inc., 1988.
36. *Lancelot of the Lake*, trans. C. Corley, Oxford University Press, 1989.
37. *Lanzalet*, trans. K.G.T. Webster, New York, Columbia University Press, 1951.

38. LAWHEAD, S., *Arthur*, Lion Books, 1989.
39. LAWHEAD, S., *Merlin*, Lion Books, 1988.
40. LAWHEAD, S., *Taliesin*, Lion Books, 1988.
41. LIEVERGOOD, B.C.J, *Mystery Streams in Europe and the New Mysteries*, New York, The Anthroposopic Press, 1982.
42. LOFFLER, C.M., *The Voyage to the Otherworld Island in Early Irish Literature*, 2 vols., Universität Salzburg, 1983.
43. LOOMIS, R.S., *The Development of Arthurian Romance*, New York, Norton, 1963.
44. LOOMIS, R.S., *The Grail From Celtic Myth to Christian Symbolism*, University of Wales Press/Columbia University Press, 1963.
45. LOOMIS, R.S., *Wales & the Arthurian Legend*, Folcroft Library Editions, 1977.
46. *The Mabinogion*, trans. Lady Charlotte Guest, The Folio Society, 1980.
47. MALORY, Sir Thomas, *Le Morte D'Arthur*, New York, University Books, 1961.
48. MARIE DE FRANCE, *Lais*, trans. G.S. Burgess and K. Busby, Harmondsworth, Penguin Books, 1986.
49. MARKALE, J., *King Arthur: King of Kings*, Gordon Cremonesi, 1977.
50. MARKALE, J., *Women of the Celts*, Gordon Cremonesi, 1975.
51. MASEFIELD, J., *Midsummer Night*, Heinemann, 1928.
52. MATTHEWS, C., *Arthur and the Sovereignty of Britain*, Arkana, 1989.
53. MATTHEWS, C., *Mabon and the Mysteries of Britain*, Arkana, 1987.
54. MATTHEWS, C., *Elements of the Celtic Tradition*, Shaftesbury, Element Books, 1989.
55. MATTHEWS, C., 'An Awesome & Splendid Thing That We Did', *Quadriga* 19 (Autumn, 1981).
56. MATTHEWS, C. & J., *The Arthurian Tarot: A Hallowquest*, Wellingborough, Aquarian Press, forthcoming, 1990.
57. MATTHEWS, J., *An Arthurian Reader*, Wellingborough, Aquarian Press, 1988.
58. MATTHEWS, J., *Elements of the Grail Tradition*, Shaftesbury, Element Books, forthcoming, 1990.
59. MATTHEWS, J., *Gawain, Knight of the Goddess*, Wellingborough, Aquarian Press, forthcoming, 1990.
60. MATTHEWS, J., *Taliesin: Shamanic Mysteries in Britain and Ireland*, Unwin Hyman, forthcoming, 1990.

61. MATTHEWS, J., 'Merlin's Esplumoir', in *Merlin and Woman*, ed. R.J. Stewart, Poole, Blandford Press 1988.

62. MATTHEWS, J. and Stewart, R.J., *Warriors of Authur*, Poole, Blandford Press, 1987.

63. MERRY, E., *The Flaming Door*, Edinburgh, Floris, 1983.

64. PATON, L.A., *Studies in the Fairy Mythology of Arthurian Romance*, New York, Franklin, 1959.

65. PAXSON, D.L., *The White Raven*, New York, William Morrow, 1988.

66. POWYS, J.C., *Porius*, Village Press, 1974.

67. *Quest of the Holy Grail*, trans. P.M. Matarasso, Penguin Books, 1969.

68. RHYS, J., *Studies in the Arthurian Legend*, Oxford University Press, 1891.

69. SHAVER, A., *Tristan and the Round Table*, New York, Medieval and Renaissance Texts & Studies, 1983.

70. SKEELES, D., *The Romance of Perceval in Prose*, Seattle, University of Washington Press, 1966.

71. SOMMER, H.O., *The Vulgate Version of the Arthurian Romances*, 7 vols., Washington, The Carnegie Institution, 1909–16.

72. STEWART, M., *The Crystal Cave*, Hodder & Stoughton, 1970.

73. STEWART, M., *The Hollow Hills*, Hodder & Stoughton, 1973.

74. STEWART, M., *The Last Enchantment*, Hodder & Stoughton, 1979.

75. STEWART, R.J. (ed.), *The Book of Merlin*, Poole, Blandford Press, 1987.

76. STEWART, R.J. (ed.), *Merlin and Woman*, Blandford Press, 1988.

77. STEWART, R.J., *The Mystic Life of Merlin*, Arkana, 1986.

78. STEWART, R.J., *The Prophetic Vision of Merlin*, Arkana, 1986.

79. STEWART, R.J. & MATTHEWS, J., *Legendary Britain*, Poole, Blandford Press, 1989.

80. SUTCLIFF, R., *The Sword at Sunset*, Hodder & Stoughton, 1963.

81. THOMAS, *Tristan in Bittany*, trans, D.L. Sayers, 1929.

82. TENNYSON, A., *Idylls of the King*, Penguin Books, 1983.

83. TOLSTOY, N., *The Quest for Merlin*, Hamish Hamilton, 1986.

84. TRAVERS, P.L., *What the Bee Knows*, Wellingborough, Aquarian Press, 1989.

85. TREECE, H., *The Great Captains*, Savoy Books, 1980.

86. VON FRANZ, M.L., *C.G. Jung: His Myth in Our Time*, Hodder & Stoughton, 1972.

87. WAY, G.L., *Fabliaux or Tales*, Rodwell, 1815.
88. WESTON, J.L., 'The Esplumoir of Merlin', *Speculum* (1946).
89. WESTON, J.L., *The Legend of Sir Perceval*, David Nutt, 1909.
90. WHITE, T.H., *The Once and Future King*, Collins, 1958.
91. WHITE, T.H., *The Book of Merlyn*, Collins, 1978.
92. WILLIAMS, C., *Taliesin Through Logres, The Region of the Summer Stars, Arthurian Torso*, Michigan, Eerdmans, 1974.

ARTHURIAN JOURNALS AND SOCIETIES

The rates quoted are correct at the time of publication. Please send an SAE or international reply-paid coupon for further details.

Quondam et Futurus, Mildred Leake Day, editor, 2212 Pinehurst Drive, Gardendale, AL 35071, USA. (This Arthurian quarterly is an independent newsletter. $10 a year for four issues in US. Overseas subscription $20, includes airmail.)

Avalon to Camelot, Freya Reeves Lambides, PO Box 6236, Evanston, IL 60204, USA. (Arthurian quarterly, illustrated, ranging from the scholarly to the worlds of media and fiction. $20 a year for four Issues in US.)

The International Arthurian Society, Secretary/Treasurer Dr Geoffrey Bromiley, Dept of French, Univ. of Durham, Elvet Riverside, New Elvet, Durham DHI 3JT. (This is the main Arthurian society in the world to which all Arthurian scholars subscribe. It holds a biennial conference and produces a bibliographical bulletin every year.)

INDEX

Agravain 95
Apple Trees, The 18
Arawn 43, 44
Arthur 42, 43, 50, 51, 52, 57,78, 80, 95
   as Celtic hero xii, 1, 7
   as Dux Brittanorum 2
   chivalric 28
   in the modern world, 84ff.
Avalon xii, 74ff
   Dwellers in, 80
Avalach 77

Balin le Sauvage, 66
Ban of Benwick 50
Bedivere 95
Blake, William, 85
Blaise 96
Boorman, John 90
Bors 96
Bran the Blessed 7, 64, 96
Brangaine 54
Brisen 97

Celts 49

Chrétien de Troyes xii, 5, 45, 59, 64, 65–6, 68
Courtly Love xii, 57
Culhwch and Olwen 6, 7

Dagonet 97
Diana 21
Dindraine xii, 70, 97
dragons 15
Dream of Rhonabwy 9
Drustan 49

Ector 97
Elaine of Astolat xii
Elaine of Corbenic 51, 53, 69, 97
Excalibur 10
Excalibur 90

Fair Unknown 44
Faery Queen 85
Frankland, Edward 87

Galahad xii, 50, 52, 68, 69, 70, 98

Galahaut 51
Gareth xii, 98
Gawain xii, 8, 23, 28, 31, 42, 43, 44, 48, 53, 75, 98
Gawain & Dame Ragnall 42
Gawain & the Green Knight 40–1, 42
Geoffrey of Monmouth 3, 5, 13, 40,77, 78
Gesta Regum Britanniae 78
Goddess 38, 42, 46, 50, 67
Gorlois 98
Gottfried von Strassbourg 58, 59
Grail xii, 10, 19, 33, 34, 51, 52, 58, 60, 62ff, 76
Green Knight 40
Gromer Somer Joure 42, 99
Guinevere xii, 8, 28, 31, 43, 51, 52, 53, 56, 69, 99
  false, 8, 51

Heath-Stubbs, John 89

Igraine 2, 99
Isolt xii, 54, 56, 99

Jamshid 64
Jones, David 87

Kay 100
Knight, Gareth 88

Lady of the Fountain 32
Lailoken 20, 21
Lamorack xii
Lancelot xii, 6, 8, 43, 48ff., 100
Lanzelet 49
Launfal 31
Lewis, C.S. 88
Life of Gildas 43

Lot of Orkney 100
Lunet 45
Lynette 45
Lyonesse 53

Mabinogion xiv, 6, 9, 43, 49
Maidens of the Wells 49
Malory xiv, 8, 22, 34, 39, 52–3, 57 58, 69, 70, 87
Marie de France 33
Mark 54, 56, 57, 100
Markale, Jean 7, 59, 80
Masefield, John 88
Matter of Britain xiii
Melwas 44
Merlin xii, 2, 13ff., 28, 39, 101
Milton, John 85
Mordred 10, 42, 52, 101
Morgan le Fay 38ff., 77, 78, 101
Morold 54, 102
Morrois, forest of 54, 58

Nimue 21, 102

Orkney clan 33
Otherworld 31, 59, 74, 75, 76, 77, 78–9
  women of xii, 46
Owein 102

Palomides 102
Pelles 51, 102
Pellinore 28, 102
Perceval xii, 66, 102
Preiddeu Annwn 7, 33, 49

Questing Beast 32

Ragnall 42, 46, 103
Robert de Borron 19, 34, 68
Round Table 27ff., 35, 50, 55

knights of xii, 2, 30, 33, 46,
    67, 70–71, 77, 80
  oath of 30
  of the Stars 80

Saxons 2
sex 49
Sone de Nausay 75–6
Sovereïgnty 6, 9, 42
Stewart, R.J. 20
Stewart, Mary, 88
Stonehenge 16
Sutcliff, Rosemary 87

Tale of Sir Gareth 44–5
Taliesin 18, 20
Tennyson, Alfred 85
Tolkein, J.R.R. 88

Tor 28
Treece, Henry, 87
Triads 49
Tristan 48ff., 103
troubadours 57, 59
Tudors 85

Uther Pendragon 2, 16, 103

Vita Merlini 13, 17, 21, 39
Vortigern 13, 104
Vulgate Cycle 21, 68, 70, 87

Wace 5
Waite, E.A. 90
White, T.H. 87–88
Williams, Charles 69, 88–89

Yeats, W.B. 90